Bernadette Halpin

28 January 2014

exhibition at the Serpentine Gallery-

Wael Shawky

Koenig Books

Horsemen Adore Perfumes and other stories

SERPENTINE GALLERIES

SHARJAH ART FOUNDATION

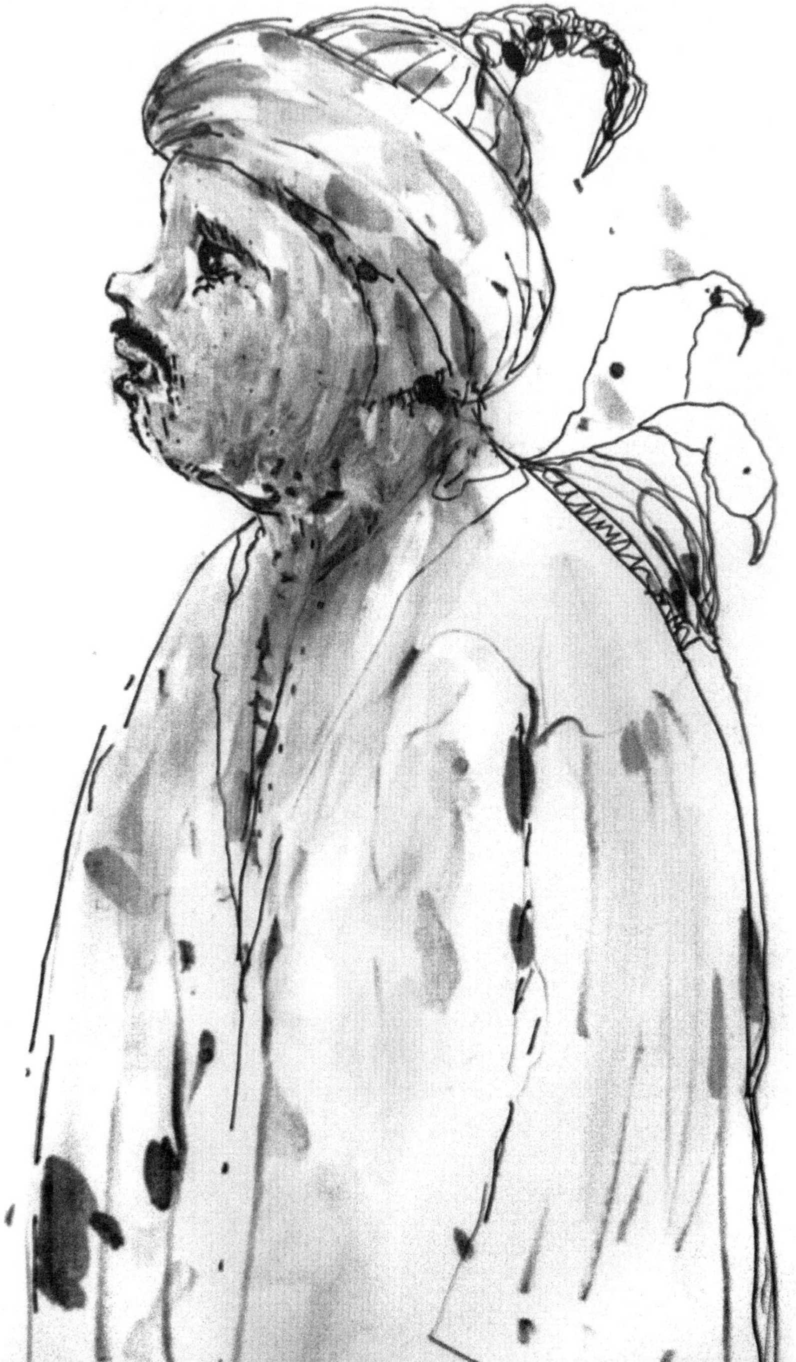

"Impart to us your last words, Father!"
But the Great Jabir continued to stare
into the distance in silence.

Mohamed Mustagab

Contents

Foreword

Julia Peyton-Jones
Hans Ulrich Obrist

This book has been jointly produced by the Sharjah Art Foundation and Serpentine Galleries on the occasion of Wael Shawky's exhibitions, opening at the Serpentine Gallery in London in 2013 and in Sharjah in 2014. This fascinating and timely focus on Shawky's work has been made possible by the partnership between the two institutions and our relationship with the artist, which has developed over the course of several years and in multiple forms. Shawky has participated in group exhibitions – 'On the Edgware Road' at the Serpentine in 2012, in the Sharjah Biennial 11 in 2013, and 'Disorientation II' which was co-produced by Sharjah Art Foundation in 2009 – and in 2011 he was invited by both our organisations to undertake a residency.

The latest episode in this collaboration is the worldwide premiere of Shawky's latest film. Shown for the first time in both the UK and Sharjah, *Al Araba Al Madfuna II* (2013), which was co-produced by the Sharjah Art Foundation and Wiener Festwochen, is at the heart of both institutions' exhibitions. This thought-provoking work is the culmination of many of the themes addressed by the artist throughout his practice and is the second in a series of films inspired by Egyptian writer Mohamed Mustagab. These films, *Al Araba Al Madfuna* (2012) and *Al Araba Al Madfuna II*, introduce Mustagab's writing to a wider international audience and the inclusion of his stories in this book will, we hope, provide readers with a deeper understanding of the significance of the narrative sources employed by Shawky in his films, drawings and installations.

Shawky's earlier *Cabaret Crusades* films, included in the Serpentine Gallery exhibition alongside his new work, also draw on a text as their source material, Lebanese writer Amin Maalouf's *The Crusades through Arab Eyes*, and employ marionettes to enact specific episodes from the holy wars. These films also involve the retelling of stories relevant to the history and culture of Shawky's native Egypt and the wider Middle East. However, in the *Al Araba Al Madfuna* series, the players are children rather than marionettes, their dubbed voices and false moustaches hinting at Shawky's intention to make the viewer question the degree to which we should adhere to received wisdom. Along with his drawings, a new series of which we are delighted to include in this book as illustrations specially produced for this project, Shawky's marionettes and installations create worlds that are often faintly surreal; places in which truth, myth and lived experiences overlap.

Shawky's varied practice, which includes performance, film and installations, communicates profound and critical observations about Arabic traditions and culture. He has rightly received international acclaim for his repeated engagement with the processes and consequences of storytelling among local and global communities alike. When asked about his interest in history books and stories, Shawky told us, 'I'm fascinated by this idea of translating history. I don't believe in history that much… I'm not stating that there is a truth or a lie. It's just another way of seeing things'. It is this element of his work that provides the focus for the exhibitions and for this book, which takes its form from both Arabic and English conventions of literary fiction. In addition to Mustagab's stories, we are delighted to include an insightful and very personal text by Hoor Al-Qasimi, President of the Sharjah Art Foundation, which introduces the reader both to Shawky's use of storytelling and to the context of this tradition in the Middle East. We are indebted to her for her commitment and dedication.

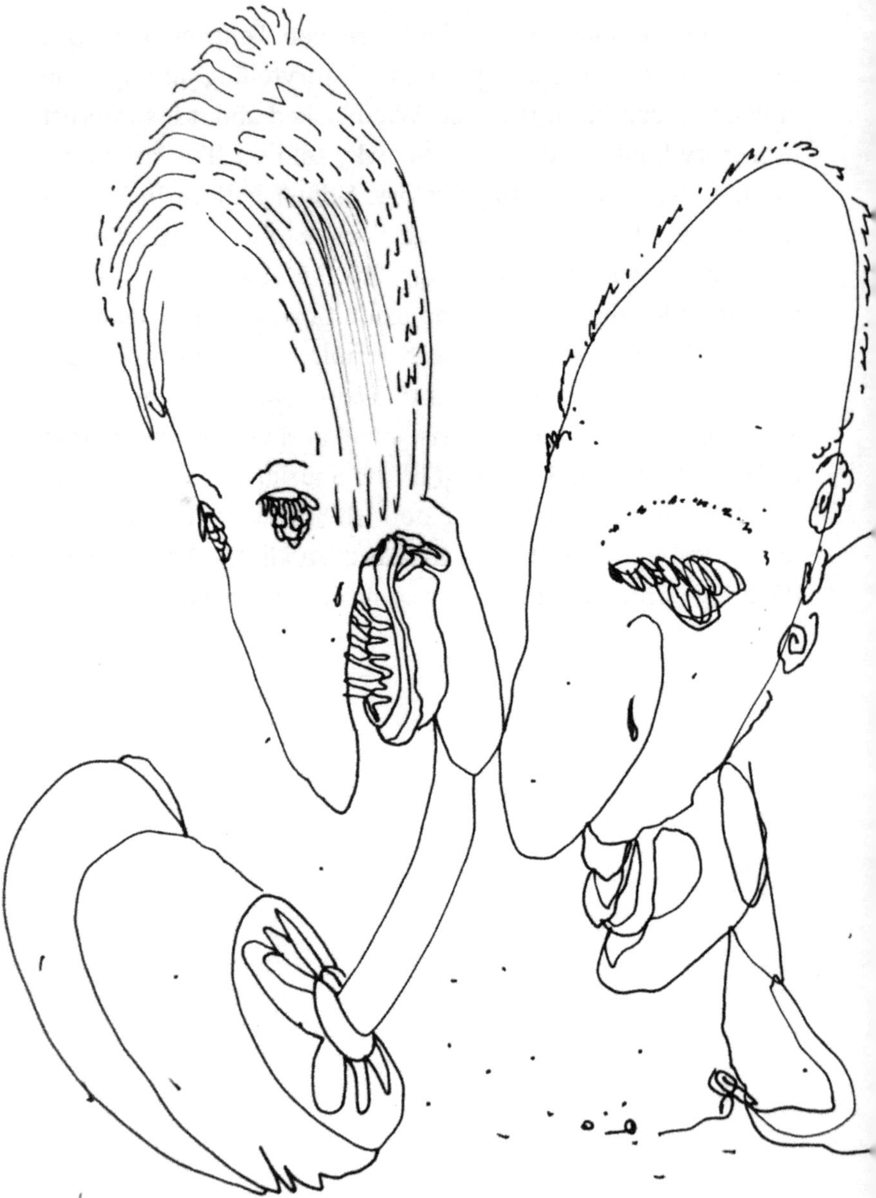

Recite/ Recount

Hoor Al-Qasimi

Growing up in an Arab family and having a historian and writer for a father, we would often hear many stories. Stories from my father's childhood, historical stories and old myths and tales, my father often uses references to these stories in the screenplays and books he writes. Storytelling is a big part of Arab culture, as it is for many cultures. Based on values, stories memorised by heart are passed down from generation to generation to shape the foundation of a society and deliver a message of unity, often at spiritual and ceremonial functions. Once the message is delivered, the story usually ends. As cycles of the tale are told and retold, different strands emerge or shift, showing various outcomes for a person's actions. In oral traditions, stories are kept alive by being told again and again and the details naturally undergo changes and adaptations during this process.

Stories tend to be seen as the work of an individual rather than a collective effort. In most of Wael Shawky's films the actors are grouped into communities and societies, and as a result, question the relevance of the author. Used as a method to demonstrate ethics and values as well as cultural norms and differences, the films are set in social environments, providing real life examples of how knowledge is applied and transferred in a social context. As we see in *Al Araba Al Madfuna* (2012), the boys take turns narrating the story. In this case, it is not only the listener who learns; the teller himself becomes more aware of his own particular circumstances. This process of storytelling is especially empowering if the teller effectively conveys ideas and, with practice, is able to demonstrate the potential of human accomplishment. The story taps into existing knowledge and can create bridges towards a solution.

Shawky uses Arabic literature and historic moments as sources of inspiration and subject matter in order to demonstrate different ways to recite and recount stories. The main source for the scripts for the film series *Al Araba Al Madfuna* was three short stories by Mohamed Mustagab (1938-2005). Shawky had been thinking of ways to adapt the Egyptian novelist's work for over fifteen years. When asked why he wanted to work with his stories, Shawky explained, 'Mustagab is interested in narrating history. He mixes religion and life to create stories that seem believable, but you know are mythical. His language establishes a link between metaphysics and physics. [Mustagab's stories] explore the way people employ metaphysical systems, like magic or the Quran, to understand the material world'.

In this respect, Shawky also becomes an alchemist, filming one story while another is being narrated. Two systems working in parallel – children speaking with the voices of adults as you hear one story while you see another story being acted out in front of you – demand focused and prolonged engagement on the part of the viewer. In both *Al Araba Al Madfuna* and *Al Araba Al Madfuna II* (2013), the settings and stories are based on Shawky's experiences in villages in Upper Egypt and the stories he heard while he was living there.

Al Araba Al Madfuna tells Mustagab's story, *The J-B-Rs*, about the gathering of a tribe, the Jabirs, who are waiting for the final counsel of the dying Great Jabir, which they then obey without question. The film is set in a real Egyptian village located close to the excavation site of Osirion in the ancient city of Abydos. Inhabitants of this village have spent years looking for treasure, digging in search of tunnels that they hope will lead to buried pharaonic chambers. Shawky's film opens with children dressed as grown men gathering in an underground space and speaking in adult voices. One of them is digging in the centre of the room, echoing the actions of the inhabitants of the real village, while the others gather to tell Mustagab's tale. The story is repeated several times, with successive Great Jabirs advising their people to get a different animal each time and the story ends when the villagers are asked to get a pig, an animal whose consumption is forbidden in Islam. This presents them with a dilemma: if they live with pigs as they did with donkeys, or eat the flesh of the pigs as they had with camels, would they eventually resemble pigs as they did when they lived with and ate camels? Each tale has the same essential narrative structure with an identifiable beginning, middle and end, but the abrupt ending encourages the viewer to assume that the villagers will repeat the same actions now with the pigs. The J-B-Rs are caught in an endless and repetitive process that results each time in failure, disappointment and distress.

In *Al Araba Al Madfuna II*, Shawky uses two stories by Mustagab that also use repetition: *The Offering* and *Horsemen Adore Perfumes*. The latter tells the story of a beautiful enchantress, hated by the villagers for her 'bloody gorging on the livelihoods of the poor'. She invites a horseman who is meant to be seeking vengeance on her to discuss matters and instead they end up marrying, which is cause for celebration by the villagers. Four days later, she emerges from her palace dragging his perfumed body and holding his severed head. This scenario is repeated a number of times with different horsemen throughout the story. *The Offering* recounts the history of a village where the inhabitants rely on the power of language to make their livings and are forced to look for more and more outlandish methods of healing themselves before finding new ways of surviving when, for no apparent reason, they are struck dumb.

In both films, the children speak in classical Arabic, a form that is rarely, if ever, spoken in social circumstances. It is seen as the voice of authority and tradition, used in literature, teachings, the Quran and news reports. The children do not necessarily understand what they are reciting, but with their narrator-like voices, they represent authority and believability, which augments the issues they are discussing. For Shawky, children are uninhibited and therefore perform less, making his characters become more real and believable. Shawky seems to use this universal approach of storytelling to bridge cultural and generation divides.

Marionnettes serve the same purpose in Shawky's film series *Cabaret Crusades* (2010 and 2012). Re-enacting the history of the crusades, a story inspired by Amin Maalouf's *The Crusades Through Arab Eyes*, the marionettes carry out their roles without exaggeration and with child-like innocence. In his *Telematch* series (2007-2009) Shawky looks at political and social changes from the times of Egyptian presidents Gamal Abd Al Nasser and Anwar Sadat to Hosni Mubarak. He attempts to capture a system or a society in transition, often using landscapes to represent the hybridity between modern Egypt and the tribal-nomad society, from rural agricultural settings to supermarkets.

Shawky's work often captures moments, settings or social practices that include a type of inversion: significant texts are translated into different languages; age and authority become hybridised; and the separation between religious and social rituals is blurred. He is interested in how history is rewritten, documented and interpreted. By translating a book into a visual form, he distils meaning from the author's work. This often leaves the viewer wondering about the author's identity, his political views, religion, ethnicity, psychology or other biographical and personal attributes. Shawky explains, 'Even if I don't believe in history I try to use written history as a way to analyse history, by being very accurate, by using the exact phrase'. An example of this can be found in Shawky's use of medieval writer Usama ibn Munqith's words in *Cabaret Crusades: The Path to Cairo*, and in works like *The Cave* (2005), where Shawky reads passages of the Quran, so the viewer can discover a 'theological' meaning, the 'message' of God. When commenting on why religion is important to his work, Shawky says, 'It was part of my childhood. I was very affected by the power of language. When religion is mixed with life, it always produces the same outcome: there is this inkling that there is something we don't believe'. This inkling is inscribed in literature and the language of history.

All quotes are taken from an interview between Wael Shawky and the author conducted in October 2013.

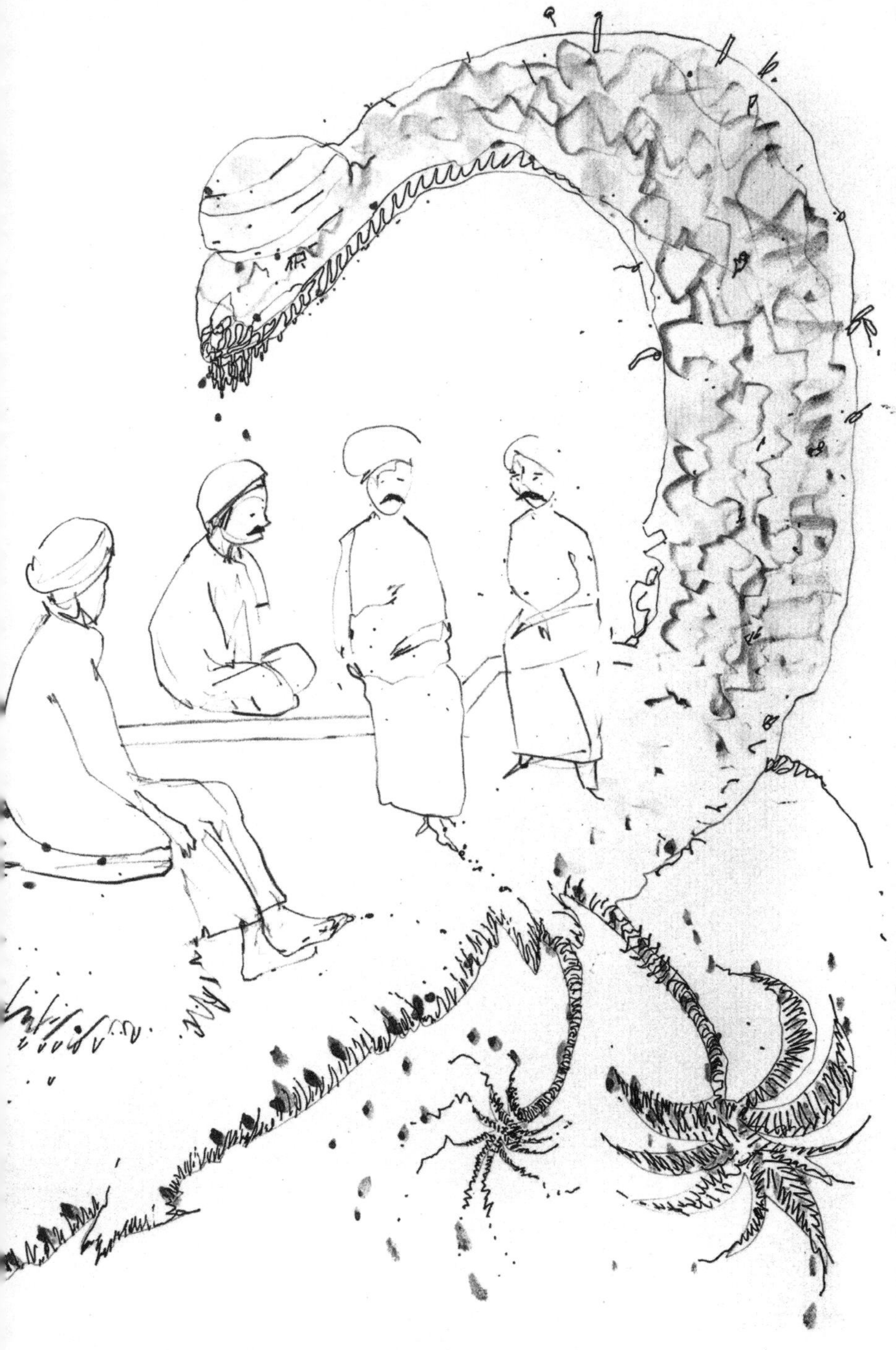

Horsemen Adore Perfumes and other stories

Mohamed Mustagab

The Offering

We do not know exactly when it happened, but that it happened is certain. My father talked of it and my mother didn't deny it, and Yahya Haqqi, Yusuf Idris, Khalil Isa al-Ghar, Ali al-Juhayni, the Khwaja Bisada, the sainted Bibawi, and Abd al-Waddud the Nasal all went on about it. Abd al-Waddud the Nasal was the most emphatic in his insistence that it really happened, but it was Yusuf Idris who made the desperate efforts to pin down the period in which it occurred, and was even so bold as to state once that what happened had happened a long time ago, in the days of the plagues that engulfed Sodom and Gomorrah, to be precise.

Despite which we do not—in this present era of ours—possess any clear evidence that, if examined, would enable us to specify the time exactly. Were Sheikh Ali, the erudite scholar of the village, still alive, he would provide us with something to base ourselves on, for Sheikh Ali possessed a book with yellow pages and protected by spells which, it is said, the village had passed down secretly from hand to hand until it ended up in his keeping. It is also said that Sheikh Ali was burned to death while the book was in his possession. Indeed, it is said that the sheikh died as a result of his attempts to unravel those spells that concealed all the details we wanted to know. It is further said (and how many are the things that are said!) that the celebrated sheikh's spirit-sister took the village's spellbound book with her to her own village, behind the blue mountains, at the place where the sun sets.

I do not deny that what my folk differed over most was the time, the starting point, and the place of occurrence. Some believe that the South Side (where the mosque, tomb, and grave marker of Amir Sinan are situated) would be the most appropriate place for the beginning, others that the North Side (with the church, tomb, and grave marker of Amba Serapion) would be more so. A third party, mostly consisting of kinship groups foreign to the town, asserts that what happened started in the centre of the town (where the houses of assignation, the brothels, the belly-dancing troupes, and the Ghawazee bands are concentrated).

No one, however, be he from the South, North, or Centre, has ever tried—and this is a fact—to deny the happening itself.

1

The happening itself began at noon on a Friday (according to the account of Abd al-Waddud the Nasal).

Or on the morning of an Easter Saturday (according to the account of the sainted Bibawi).

A man from my village was sitting at the top end of his field intoning one of our celebrated songs of patience when his tongue became heavy and began to trip. The man became confused and panic-stricken. He had not become completely dumb, but the words that had been pouring from his larynx had lost their fluidity. They were ravaged in the depths of his throat and emerged as though crushed in a mill—mere letters, joined together by nothing but a stammering wail, stretched and taut.

The man stayed where he was, alone, trying to mould the sounds emerging from his throat. His lips, tongue, pharynx, the inner muscles of his cheek, and his palate struggled to link the letters, correct the words, order the particles, and beat the phonetic mob into submission, but in vain.

The man rushed to his house, his horror tucked under his arm—and not just under his arm, for he had also bitten off a great mouthful of it that was knocking about in his mouth and forcing yellow pallor, terror, and dread into his whole being.

My village rushed to stand by its son. Some appeared to practice magic and break the spell. Some arrived to bleed his brain and the place between his shoulders. Some came to take a piece of the afflicted man's clothing so they could burn it for their barren wives to step over seven times, after which these same wives would bathe on a moonlit night in water containing a frog with its throat slit. And some were there to explain the whole event away and pin it on the unbelief that had defiled the life of the sick man and caused him to abandon his religion and stop visiting the tombs of the saints.

But my village is fickle. It broke into commotion, it screamed, it offered solace, and it declared its opinion. Then it left things up to the one concerned, returning to its quarters convinced that what had happened had had to happen, for every now and then someone had to get bitten by a scorpion, or drown in the river, or have a wall collapse on him, or fall out of a palm tree, or meet our famous afreet Hawwash, who would terrify him into paralysis, or the Waterwheel Girl, who would corner him and scoop him up and carry him off with her to the well of a waterwheel or the cavity under a weir. Yes indeed, my village is fickle and it knows full well that it must, from time to time, play host to an event of this nature, when a certain predetermined percentage of its men has to be presented as an offering to fate—and thereafter let all not thus afflicted praise God.

In this way my village was able to satisfy itself as to the significance of the event before placing its arm beneath its head and going to sleep.

Things did not, however, stop with the dumbness of a single man. By the end of that same day a donkey trader had lost the power of speech without even having left his house, that his way might be blocked by the afreet Hawwash or the Waterwheel Girl.

Before the village could recover from its fear, an observant woman was struck dumb, and on the East Side a snake bit the tongue of the market supervisor, and the tongue of a statue maker was split in two. Five, six, sixty, a hundred, the whole village—even the pious preacher of its mosque, a man as white-hearted as milk and as kind as the prophet, a man as demure as a virgin, as gallant as a knight, and as brave as Ibn Abi Talib, this eloquent preacher opened his mouth as wide as it would go, there where he stood in the pulpit urging the believers to be patient, abandon sin, and cleave unto the ropes of the Creator—and his mouth stayed open. When the congregation noticed, they rushed to him and carried him away in an atmosphere of terror and affright that was filled with their mewings, croakings, and consternation.

Appeals had to be made to God and lips to be smacked in dismay.

But my village had been struck dumb. Its tongue had become paralyzed, the scales on it dissolving, and it could no longer form any of those mighty letters that make up speech. The village was struck dumb. Dismay afflicted its body and dizziness its head. Its eyes opened wide in terror. The disease had come upon it and it rushed right and left, importuning the houses of the saints and the tombs of the sheikhs and Allies of God, pounding mustard, fenugreek, sea ambrosia, lemongrass, and galangal and making out of them a concoction to drink on an empty stomach after rising, making a detour to the tombs where it sucked up the dirt, and then descending into the depths of the canals and water outlets to bathe or anoint its body with mud, pleading with the Lord at candle-lit altars and then praying every morning the two prostrations of the Prayer against Fright, cutting palm fronds and weaving them into crosses beneath which to sleep on moonlit nights and then pulling the crosses to pieces and rushing to the courtyard of the mosque to wail and call on the Only, the Victorious—all in an attempt to outmanoeuvre its terrible malady but ending up outmanoeuvred by it. For it would return to itself only to find the dumb impossible still balled up in its mouth and itself still powerless to marshal letter beside letter, order word after word, and failing, at the end of the day, to form a sentence. Or if, on rare occasions, it succeeded in marshalling letter next to letter and ordering word after word, it would discover that the sentence it had arrived at was not the sentence it had sought, but a shredded, smashed, fragmented, truncated speech that dribbled from wide open mouths within which a tongue of cold, soft, flesh lay prostrate in a lake of spittle.

Toilsome were the efforts they expended to arrive at the secret of the calamity and to diagnose the disaster. They approached certain people of knowledge and miracles in the surrounding areas and slaughtered sheep and turkeys in their honour. They suffered the swallowing or chewing of amulets and were forced to jump over circular pits of fire fuming with incense, rats' tails, and insects' legs. They sought the help of the gypsies and Bedouin who passed their way, and the village filled with quacks and magicians, people with second sight and others who kept company with devils. And when their tribulation remained unchanged, delegations journeyed to Kordofan, Siwa, and Wadi al-Masakhit. Each returned with his own explanation and justification: a ruling from the oases said that someone in the village must, beyond any doubt, have sinned with his mother or father; according to another report, someone from the village must have practiced the Shameful Act on sacks of wheat, so that the blessed staff of life itself had become angry.

I should mention finally that among the attempts to undo the spell cast upon the village was one that required the slaughter of a red-headed orphan and the smearing of his blood on the buttocks of the men and the inner thighs of the women. When the village actually prepared this cure using a child they had abducted from a neighbouring hamlet, and when the neighbouring hamlet discovered that its red-headed orphan had gone missing, and after it came to their knowledge that he had been transformed into a potion to cure the village of dumbness, the furious people of the hamlet surrounded the village and entered it by force, slaughtering a number of its sons and menfolk, insulting eight of its women, and urinating on the faces of a hundred of its elders, with the result that my village desisted from testing further solutions.

2

Dismay continued to press down upon the breast of my village, silently, savagely, wildly. True, the fields dried up and poverty and yellowness afflicted them. True, the paintwork on the houses cracked and mud bricks fell from the sides of the door frames. True, the animals aborted and their udders went dry. And true, dust stained the people's faces, beards, and turbans. But none of that, none of it at all, was what mattered to my village. What mattered was its tongue.

My village was in no way whatsoever involved in manual labour. It was a trading village, all of whose elders and leading men were merchants—merchants in calves, buffaloes, chickens, bran and flour siftings, honey, grains, and vegetables. They depended above anything else on that jewel of a muscle, the tongue. With their tongues they paid compliments, argued, enticed, and invoked the Living, Eternal God and the holy books, and with their tongues they praised, lied, slandered, defended, and whiled away the evenings in agreeable converse. It was a flexible, mobile, tongue that remained constantly at play inside their mouths until that moment when it would pull out the appropriate sentence, whisper the loveliest, most radiant, and most delicate words, and spit out the harshest and most abominable utterances. It would sniff and savour, this ancient tongue, and roam and tour in the markets and at weddings, and then return to the houses with the most ample profits; a tongue sweet and responsive at whose singing every body in the area started to dance—fluent, super-exquisite, smooth, glad, a tongue that wriggled in the depths of wisdom, legend, and story. How many lands and cities did Abu Zayd, through the tongue of my village, invade, and conquer! Over how many walls and to the foot of how many battlements did Mercurial Ali, using the same means, leap, to disappear or to stand and fight! How far did Hasan the famous troubadour wander in search of his Na'ima, the tongue of my village unrolling before him plains and valleys that he might be carefree and sing and meet with his beloved! Even that ancient, terrifying tale, the tale of the man who murdered his brother, ripped his corpse to pieces, and scattered it throughout the region, became, on the tongue of my village, a warm and dreamy story telling of how the wife of the murdered man gathered his remains and brought them back to life.

There is no might and no power but in God. Behold our ancient tongue now retracted, shrunken, and benumbed, sleeping on the cast-off swaddling bands of speech as it lay tattered and collapsed on the floor of the throat! Behold the green songs of joy wither, the cheerful comments curdle, the laugh, once deep and broad, go flaccid, and naught but gloom and hissing remain!

3

My village remained in this state for a time—some say a month, some a year, some a hundred years—before it took a grip on itself, stiffened its resolve, dragged its exhausted body from the houses of the saints and the befrogged baths, and returned to its fields and beasts, its crops and palm trees, and all its other business. Hunger, nakedness, and the mockeries of the surrounding villages had worn it down. It had been rocked to its foundations but hastened to take charge once more of its affairs, convulsed as those might be. Arms, legs, and muscles set to work, turning ruined waterwheels, opening irrigation ditches, moving dirt, boring wells, and digging outlet channels. My village, speech-deprived, silent, and emaciated, moved toward its land, its trees, its vessels, its braziers, its ovens, and the tethering places of its animals. Loss of speech is a catastrophe, but hunger will make a man forswear his faith, and though speech be a necessity, the right of the gut takes precedence. At this point, my village started, slowly and in sorrow, to put its affairs in order again, for if the tongue had died, the other members—the eyes, arms, feet, reproductive member, heart, and brain—remained alive and in working order and it was the job of the tongue to allow its energy and powers to seep into the rest of the body's substance. Thus my village resorted to our first, primitive, ancient language, dusting it off and restoring it to pristine newness and returned to the sign and the art of the sign, that curious, ancient art, that solution held in reserve for any crisis the tongue may face.

The village began to develop the effectiveness of sign language. True, it might mew, croak, and make drawn out sounds, but it was through movements of the hands, the eyebrows, and the mouth, and noddings of the head, that it was able to forget, or pretend to forget. In any case, it moved. It moved away from the memory of the first days of its trial and that before its powers of speech had withered completely away, as soon, indeed, as it became clear that he who could produce a properly formed sentence was no better off than he who could produce only a mangled one. In any case, it moved. It moved to its beasts, to take them out into the open air, to its crops and trees, to help their growth and tend them, to its houses, to rebuild their collapsing walls, and to its mudbrick benches, to remove them entirely from before the doorways, for there was no longer any reason for people to keep company with one another of an evening. Soon mosques with no minarets appeared on the skyline, for the people had substituted for the exhortatory voice mere bangings on metal sheets or drums to call men to the performance of the mandated prayers. Next it was the turn of the eyes and ears to assume a new importance, and it became a duty to listen carefully for the lightest of light hisses, to be alert to the slightest of slight movements. They busied themselves with the art of the sign, improving it and inventing new gestures, not just for rapid communication when haste was imperative, but also for the telling of stories. My village became capable, even, of recounting the tales of wonder, such as those of the Man with the Flayed Leg, the She-ghoul, Clever Hasan, and Thimble and the Moon of All Moons. Indeed, it reached a point where the two arms could reproduce, in miniature, all the effects of the tongue and even tell jokes, puzzles, riddles, and funny stories, and there came a time when my village used to tell—yes, tell—stories that included anecdotes about a man who could speak, just as nowadays we might tell an anecdote about a man who was dumb.

4

The fields and the river banks revived despite the withering of the tongue, but the village's trade lay fallow. Certainly, you might do business once, for example, with a trader who couldn't speak, but you would not be able to deal on a permanent basis with all the speechless traders of the village. True, the traders attempted to compensate with their hands for what their tongues were incapable of making plain, but trade has another side, one that calls for whispers and shouts, persuasion and concession. My village might not have taken very long to return to its fields, but it was totally incapable of returning to the world of trade, for the fields, in the end, were under their owners' control, whereas in trade the villagers were only one party, and a party that found the greatest difficulty in convincing the other parties to do business with it, especially when those other parties were the rival villages that crowded the broad river valley and with which my village had clashed when it slaughtered the red-headed orphan.

Many are the reports that have come down to us on this matter. It is rumoured, for example, that the traders' businesses failed and that the traders then melted into the mass of peasants and were assimilated among them, becoming landowners, renters, or day labourers. It was also claimed that the traders were transformed into simple middlemen, whose modest aspirations were limited to the villagers' internal dealings, and likewise, by way of further example, that the traders abandoned their village and infiltrated themselves into other distant villages far from one another, each of which was capable of supporting a single dumb trader. All of this meant that our village set sail for the shore, seeking for itself other affairs that were in harmony with any road it might take.

It is said that my village, having been deprived of its evening gatherings and convivial assemblies and finding difficulty in communicating its stories and scandals, its complaints and individual adventures, was compelled to invent other gatherings that did not employ the tongue, gatherings that had their own special means of providing pleasure. The tongue had withered away and its sound had been silenced, true enough; but the village took refuge in the palms of hands—the palms of its own hands. It was slow work at first and palm continued to strike palm only in order to announce certain small affairs—to call someone, or to denote approval or disapproval or refusal or anger. Then, quickly, the palms devised for themselves a special form of clapping that was comfortable and entertaining. A brand new art, the art of clapping, began to enter the blood and marrow of the village and take the place of songs, stories, evening discourse, curious anecdotes, and everything else for which recourse had been made to speech, letters, words, opinions, and argument. My village found itself realizing itself in clapping, in its variegation, until this came to constitute sufficient raw material for its entertainment, and nightly gatherings and parties were held that were based thereon. The village might seek the assistance of a singer from outside, but there can be no doubt that merriment, joy, and social cohesion had their source in those unerring, artistic, well-schooled palms. Indeed, with time, it became an easy thing to hold an evening party without a singer at all, the dancer gliding into the midst of a circle quivering to the gladdening beat of palms, a beat implanted deep in the body and heart—the beat of palms on palms, of palms on backs or on knees, on cheeks or on legs. Medleys and rhythms were born out of my village's genuine desire to enjoy itself and forget what was over and done with. There even came a time when the people of my village would invade the nocturnal gatherings and wedding parties of the other villages, despite all the constraints. And while it was possible that you might find in the other villages a gifted singer, dancer, or instrumentalist, you would certainly find that all the clappers were from mine.

Where trade failed to provide for my village, the art of clapping succeeded. A wedding would be put on in a settlement on the other side of the mountain, and the impresario would invite our people to perform. Art swept away, as it usually does, all the reservations and fears that, for a while, had constrained my village's movements, and the other villages, without exception, acknowledged the right of my village to participate in any wedding or social occasion. And it went beyond a mere matter of bands of clappers to encompass the training of the ghawazees and the selection and preparation of the most beautiful, supple, and fresh-faced of their daughters. The whole valley quivered at the magical, fetching, wordless beauty that swayed before it, freighted with everything that might arouse. The former traders, or their grandsons, or their grandsons' grandsons, found themselves at ease with this new market in whose efflorescence they were able to discover a living for themselves, and the village became crowded with bands—ghawazees, women solo dancers, players of the zummar, clappers, organizers, and impresarios—and the money flowed in, compensating them for what they had lost with the disappearance of their tongue. It no longer saddened the village that its mouth had been transformed into nothing more than an empty cavity seeking nourishment, or a thing with which they did no more than breathe. What had been absurd and shameful became, in this new dispensation, an advantage and a sign of distinction, and the mansions of the traders of the villages of the valley filled with men and women from my village who worked for them as guardians and nannies of their children. These would keep the secrets of the houses and preserve their privacy. They alone were the witnesses, but their mouths were sealed, incapable of revealing anything that might do the family harm, lower its prestige, or bring it shame.

5

The new businesses brought my village to the peak of its resurgence. The time when its sons and daughters worked as hired performers at weddings and soirées ended. Instead they began to negotiate their own contracts for the organization of festivities such as these and others recently invented. The village became intoxicated with its squares, which blossomed with joy, dancing, clapping, and fun. In no time, the weddings and good times swung out of the houses, squares, and streets and took to the fields. Some families grew famous for providing the most sumptuous food, others for providing the most splendid dancers, and yet others for hosting the costliest and most luxurious events. The village awoke to the value of its grapes and dried them and distilled them. It squeezed its sugarcane and fermented it. It dug long burrows beneath the houses and stored in these vaults beer and arak from Zahle. Certain particularly gifted individuals were able to create numerous recipes for the enhancement of sexual potency. Hashish and opium became widespread and were grown over wide swathes of village land. The houses became too small for any gatherings or soirées and were reserved only for sleeping and making things. Pleasure took place in the open air, outside the green, silent village, in places where tents, shacks, and gorgeous chalets were erected. The wheat did its best to grow, but the market for it had gone and so it joined the rice and the corn, which stole into the canal bottoms and tried to sprout in out-of-the-way corners. It was not long, however, before our village took a stand against this infiltration and forbade the planting of crops that might exhaust the soil in a celebrated law that enumerated these crops, among which were wheat and corn, rice and beans. Nor did the law omit to encourage plants with a long-term positive impact on the existing economy (on which, see the story "Sunflowers").

Some of those concerned with the development of the village during this period claim that this transformation created numerous victims, but I can assure you here that the number of those in my village who suffered during this critical phase could be counted on one's fingers and toes, plus the fingers and toes of the neighbours, and that when these bad-mouthers say 'victims' they mean those lazy peasants and riffraff whose capacities could take them no further than the sowing of crops which the village no longer needed. It is true that some converted to crops whose importance and necessity had become obvious, but many—and these were the ones who suffered—insisted on sowing cereals. Some of them tried to get around the law that forbade them and encouraged the sowing of 'fancies' by planting wheat clandestinely in among the sunflowers, and the authorities were obliged to strip the land bare, plot by plot, in order to clean the village holdings of every planting they held to be injurious. Some people they sent to trial: a peasant in whose field a number of lentil plants were seized was sent to jail, and a family was banished and all its members expelled from the village (Case No. 1033 B) because they had organized a gang for smuggling seed beans, and there was a number of other diverse cases which there is no need to enumerate here.

Such limited albeit significant issues aside, our village had nothing to worry about. The hostile forces retreated in the face of progress, those besotted with the toilsome life of the family were defeated, and certain individuals were brought low. Thereafter the village discovered the true path to happiness with none to oppose it and laboured to further embellish its offerings and streamline its affairs, courting the neighbouring villages by constantly sending out delegations to advertise and announce the village's new attractions in the way of the pleasures and relaxations available to any who spent a holiday in one of its luxurious chalets.

H.G. Wells says in his book The Outline of History (Book

VI, p. 660), "The abodes of the 'harem' and of luxury were full to bursting with slave girls, dancers, jesters, actors, go-betweens, and guards, all clustering around the patrons and the rich, endeavouring to gain the favour of the guests—that favour which filled the nests with feathers, the coffers with gold, and minds with pleasure."

Outside the village, time came to a stop and refused to breach its walls, which must give us cause to re-evaluate the meaning of immortality.

6

We frequently find that we cannot easily depart from places we love, but feel a need to rove about in them. This is especially true of a village such as mine that is so well provided with the comforts of life, so decorative, so sweet-smelling, so fragrant with goodness, with colour, and with silence, such a foretaste of Paradise, so much the longed-for goal of the onlooker's eye and safe haven of his heart.

Were it not that I do not trust many of the reports that have come down to us across the long intervening ages, I would have taken you through my village house by house, chalet by chalet, for it is related that its prince (or its ruler, or its mayor, or its sharif), on waking, would drink a glass into which four or five locally raised sheep had been squeezed, that he used to keep in the house where he spent his forenoons eighteen females, and in the house where he spent his evenings thirty-six more, and that, before the village's army was disbanded, he would attend the manoeuvres of the night watchmen, watching from a tent festooned with girls. Likewise it is said that he never had an opportunity to set foot to ground, that he used to snack before sleeping on powdered hashish and sugar, and that he was just and honourable, loved truth, goodness, and beauty, and pitied the poor. It is also related that the prince, enamoured of ingénues, set aside land that he enclosed and planted with trees and shrubs, then furnished with dens and knolls, and into whose tracts he released numerous young girls, so that pleasure, in this wild and licentious atmosphere, reigned unconfined. A writer or two attempted to study this intoxicating reality, but the keeper of the papyri indicated that their writings should begin with the observation that these events had happened in past ages, before the tongue of the village had been paralyzed, and when they refused he ordered them to be thrown out and to die in exile.

The noisy, raucous, oboe-tootling, wordless parties held by the village would end before dawn to allow the patrons time to bring their previously agreed upon pleasures to a close before noon of the following day. The silent satisfaction of desire in my village reached a point at which the very dogs lost their dogginess and were transformed into no more than cheerfully yawning animals which the foxes stepped over and sometimes even dallied with. The patrons and guests would sometimes take a fancy to the idea of kidnapping the girls off the streets, jokingly or in all seriousness or in an attempt to alleviate their boredom, since this brought them (at least) a kind of pleasure. When they were taken to the prince's jail, the prince's men would offer apologies and gifts to the accused and warn the beautiful dumb girls not to cause trouble in the future. One noble act that history has confided to us concerned a man who murdered his wife for having given birth to five male children and not one female. It is said that the man buried the children alive in an opium field, and when brought to trial for his conduct offered by way of excuse his fear that his house would be reduced in the future to ruin, an excuse that the judge accepted, awarding him compensation.

Horsemen Adore Perfumes

The day shuddered and shook the nests of the little birds into the furnace of fire. Grief jumped to the left and poured dust over the bodies of the children. The cities shook with laughter, hymns, dementia, and glee. The ovens of the villages collapsed on the pots of baking food and the warming bread.

A woman who loves dogs and collects foxes said, "Beware this sour black face! It leaves sterility behind it and spreads fornication. It wrangles with the truth, smashes silk cocoons, trades in the skins of virgins, brings sadness, and feeds on adversity."

*

The day shuddered and shook the nests of the little birds into the furnace of fire. The ravens laughed long, till their feet and beaks and the tips of their wings turned white. The lower banks of the canals developed cracks where esparto, datura, and lizards grew to giant size. Ants pranced around the udders of the cows. The horseman unsheathed his blade and mounted his pitch-black steed. The children of the poor circled about him and he bestowed upon them smiles and strength of purpose, solace and sweetmeats. The horseman pushed on through the throngs, the streets, and the sorrows till he reached the palace of the Enchantress of the Age. The weather was springlike, the sorrow warm, the sadness ablaze.

"Doltish and evil Enchantress of the Age, squatting on the village throne, I am come to take vengeance for your bloody gorging on the livelihoods of the poor."

The masses charged in fury, the trees clung to the remnants of green, and the waters of the river wrestled with the cracks of the drought. The guards clung to the walls of the palace, ready to defend the enchantress. The beautiful enchantress looked down from her royal compartment, and the people exploded with ire and rocks, screams and brickbats. The enchantress, however, stood her ground unmoved. The throngs increased in tenacity and solidarity around the horseman, whose smile expanded till it embraced the sheep, the waterwheels, the children, the ovens, the masses, the songs of praise, and the songs of patience. The horseman advanced his last step, determined to close the account of the bitter years. The masses moved behind him, carrying their children on their shoulders. The enchantress made a gesture with her arm. The crowds halted. The guards closed ranks more tightly, made themselves yet readier for the annihilation of the masses. And the enchantress screamed in her furious, tender voice, "I know your demands, but beware of blood. What harm have the guards and the masses done that they should fight one another? I am prepared to investigate the matter."

*

The horseman advanced. In the forenoon the investigation began and in the evening the marriage was announced, and the masses were intoxicated with merriment and rejoicing, joy and exultation. And on the fourth day the enchantress emerged from her palace dragging behind her the body of the stubborn horseman, smeared with perfumes. She dragged him through the streets as far as the village market and in the middle of the square laid out the horseman's body, smeared with perfumes, and cut off his head.

*

Grief jumped to the left and poured dust over the bodies of the children. The cities shook with laughter, hymns, dementia, and glee. The acacias advanced, destroying the fruits of the mulberry trees. The braziers were extinguished and the dogs climbed onto the beds, the bedding, the seats. The snakes took their ease in the burrows of the rabbits. The hornets buzzed around the water butts. The poor gathered close round the bards and the storytellers, the chanters of collects and the concocters of charms. The bellies teemed with worms. The horseman's brother unsheathed his blade and mounted his pitch-black steed. The children of the poor circled about him and he bestowed upon them smiles and strength of purpose, solace and sweetmeats. The horseman pushed on through the throngs, the streets, and the sorrows till he reached the palace of the Enchantress of the Age. The weather was springlike, the sorrow warm, the sadness ablaze.

"Doltish and evil Enchantress of the Age, squatting on the village throne, I am come to take vengeance . . . ."

The enchantress made a gesture with her arm. In the forenoon the investigation began and in the evening the marriage was announced, and the masses were intoxicated with merriment and rejoicing, joy and exultation. And on the fourth day the enchantress emerged from her palace dragging behind her the body of the stubborn horseman, smeared with perfumes. She dragged him through the streets as far as the village market and in the middle of the square laid out the horseman's body, smeared with perfumes, and cut off his head.

*

The ovens of the villages collapsed on the pots of baking food and the warming bread. The mouths closed and opened and the saliva began to flow. The mind twisted to the right and to the left and then shrank back inside its skull. Sheep laid eggs, guts went dry, and rosebushes sprouted cabbages. Love jammed in lumps inside ovarian tubes. Broomrape teased the debilitated fava beans with lines of wisdom verse. An angel intimated to the Lord that He might wish to halt the farce. The horseman's son unsheathed his blade and mounted his pitch-black steed. The children of the poor circled about him and he bestowed upon them smiles and strength of purpose, solace and sweetmeats. The horseman pushed on through the throngs, the streets, and the sorrows till he reached the palace of the Enchantress of the Age. The weather was spring-like, the sorrow warm, the sadness ablaze.

"Doltish and evil Enchantress of the Age, squatting on the village throne, I am come to take vengeance . . . ."

The enchantress made a gesture with her arm. In the forenoon the investigation began and in the evening the marriage was announced, and the masses were intoxicated with merriment and rejoicing, joy and exultation. And on the fourth day the enchantress emerged from her palace dragging behind her the body of the stubborn horseman, smeared with perfumes. She dragged him through the streets as far as the village market and in the middle of the square laid out the horseman's body, smeared with perfumes, and cut off his head.

*

The clouds drooped, darkened, and complained of the absence of water. The underground vaults writhed in ruin and extended themselves into the depths of the jugulars. The woman who loves dogs and collects foxes applied herself to homilies with the angels. The horseman's grandson unsheathed his blade and mounted his pitch-black steed and in the forenoon the investigation began.

The J-B-Rs

- The voice of the J-B-Rs quivered with sorrow. The Great Jabir, laid out in his winding sheet, indicated to them with a blink of his eyelids that they should sit. One of them whispered through his tears, "Impart to us your last words, Father!" But the Great Jabir continued to stare into the distance in silence.

- Quaveringly, the voice of the clan of Jabir rose in a hymn that spoke of a vizier who started life in a pit. But the Great Jabir continued to stare into the distance in silence.

- Someone with a ringing voice chanted the tale of the one who was afflicted in his body by ulcers and whose wife carried him to the ends of the earth in search of a cure. But the Great Jabir continued to stare into the distance in silence.

- The faces of the J-B-Rs leaped from the corner to the ceiling, to the bedding, and finally to the face of the Great Jabir, which radiated light: "Impart to us your last words, Father!"

- And before the Great Jabir's eyelashes closed, he whispered forcefully, "My final counsel to you is, 'Get a camel!'"

1

A camel! And the delegations of mourners muttered, in patience and in solace, "The Lord taketh and the Lord giveth." Never had the J-B-Rs thought of a camel. One Great Jabir presided over the obsequies of another Great Jabir, and the camel roamed about, an idea that pressed down upon them as it materialized, seeping from those words of final counsel into their whispers, and every short while the mouth of one Jabir would approach the ear of another Jabir to whisper, "The Lord taketh and the Lord giveth," for as long as four-legged animals had been four-legged animals, the settlement of the Jabir clan had loved donkeys—had loved riding donkeys, shaving donkeys' hair, staining donkeys with henna, bridling donkeys, trimming donkeys' hooves, fashioning saddles and manure sacks for donkeys, doctoring donkeys' backs, and fighting sores, broken knees, and hoof rot—and there wasn't a Jabir on the face of the earth who could not tell, at a glance, the sex and age of any donkey, the number of shoes it had worn out, its hometown, and the trials and tribulations that had befallen it from the days when its hooves were still soft. The Lord taketh and the Lord giveth. A camel! Scarcely had the funeral broken up before half the J-B-Rs were convinced that Jubran the Stylite had lived thirty-five years as an ascetic and recluse on top of a pillar because the settlement was devoid of camels. A towering, imposing camel! Camels traversed the desert, carrying bread and fuel, patience and potency, to the isolated monks. Saint Garapamon had sought shelter from the midday heat in the shadow of his camel and then had slaughtered it from hunger, and the camel had wept in consent. The other half of the J-B-Rs convinced themselves that they were not like the Sons of Abd al-Capricious, who had devoted their lives to the goat, or like the Clan of the Cleidonians, who roamed the settlements repairing the locks of doors, and nor would they, from that day on, be like those notorious groups that had fallen prey to the attractions of chickens or rabbits, of peering into the future through puddles of ink, of beating drums at zar ceremonies, making amulets, and stealing shrouds from the dead, of grinding scissors and knives. A camel! Praise be, to the Lord first, and to the dear departed Jabir second!

The first camel, coming from Suakin, Samalut, the Forty-Day Road, or Siwa, appeared. With its high hump and towering neck, its head that gazed at the clouds, it towered over the settlement, and its voice, which resembled that of water gushing from a narrow-necked jug, flowed forth, calm and patient, as it slowly proceeded, placing its feet carefully to spare the ground. A wave of joy passed over the J-B-Rs and they jived and jumped, each higher than the last. A Jubayr clung to the high neck, while a Jubran climbed up the camel's hump but fell off and a Jubrana played with its short tail, so that the settlement grew in merriment and the Jabir clan swayed with energy and bliss. With every passing day, more camels made their way to the settlement, and with each new camel the J-B-Rs discovered meat, pride, and camel hair, and how much they'd suffered inside those pokey houses in their pokey alleys. So the J-B-Rs demolished the doorposts of the houses and widened them, and they strewed sand in the courtyards and plazas. A Jubayra invented a spindle which, though it made everyone laugh, produced thread from camel hair, and in the end she gathered these threads and made a scarf to go round the neck of her Jubran. Another resourceful Jabbur put together a loom and the settlement filled with camel-hair mantles, scarves, blankets, and warmth. An aged Jabara taught the young ones how to make camel litters, and the settlement was ecstatic when for the first time in its history a bride was led in procession on the back of a camel; previously—during that age of which they no longer cared to think—they had transported the bride from house to house without that extremity of joy which now shone forth: a beautifully made and decorated litter, with the bride up on top glowing and glittering, the camel swaying beneath her! Shots could ring out and it would not take fright. Ululations could erupt and it would not take fright. Fires could be lit and it would not take fright. Camels could be slaughtered—for feasting and celebration—and it would not take fright. It even reached the point that those who had got married before insisted on celebrating their nuptials all over again.

*

Over the course of a few years, the J-B-Rs got mixed up with the camels and the camels with the J-B-R-s. The ceilings of their houses were raised and they took to wearing the silken shawl, the woven headdress, and the elegant slippers. They surpassed the Bedouin in the manufacture and exquisite finishing of camel litters, and they succeeded in discovering a new compound for treating the mange. They also grew skilled at preserving cured meats for months. Two Jabirs who lived next door to one another took to storing drippings and gravy made from the bones. A Jabrun was able to corner the market in camel hides and became an expert at marketing these in the settlements that lay scattered throughout the valley. A persevering Jabra succeeded in creating treatments for vitiligo from camels' intestines and for deafness from camels' ear drums, for sleepwalking from camels' hooves, for disruptions to the menstrual cycle from camels' marrow, and for increased confidence on wedding nights from camels' penises. Then a yet more persevering Jabra succeeded in drying camel sinew, which he pounded with burned camel hair and the grease from the back of camel necks, ending up with a compound for treating sterility. Thus the settlement grew in glory, luxury, and pride until even the bodies of the J-B-Rs grew taller and their necks longer, their voices mixed with the nasal sound of water flowing from narrow-necked jugs, and their eyes grew bigger and their ears shorter. Very soon, their lips had become cleft and their feet had splayed out.

*

- The voice of the J-B-Rs quivered with sorrow. The Great Jabir, laid out in his winding sheet, indicated to them with a blink of his eyelids that they should sit. One of them whispered through his tears, “Impart to us your last words, Father!” But the Great Jabir continued to stare into the distance in silence.

- One of them hurried to collect sticks in a bundle to remind them that in unity lay strength. But the Great Jabir continued to stare into the distance in silence.

- Quaveringly, the voice of the clan of Jabir rose in a hymn that spoke of a vizier who started life in a pit. But the Great Jabir continued to stare into the distance in silence.

- Someone with a ringing voice chanted the tale of the one who was afflicted in his body by ulcers and whose wife carried him to the ends of the earth in search of a cure. But the Great Jabir continued to stare into the distance in silence.

- Someone with a sweet-toned voice recited the homily of the camel that had crossed the wide open spaces searching for the killer of its friend. But the Great Jabir continued to stare into the distance in silence.

- The face of the J-B-Rs leaped from the corners to the ceiling, to the bedding, and finally to the face of the Great Jabir, which radiated light: “Impart to us your last words, Father!”

- And before the Great Jabir's eyelashes closed, he whispered forcefully, "My final counsel to you is, 'Get a mule!'"

2

A settlement pure as pure can be, of men from pure loins. How could it be that it had never occurred to them to get a mule? The moment it had finished receiving condolences for the loss of the Great Jabir, the settlement began to look askance at the kneeling camels with their huge bulk, their stupid eyes, and their twisty necks. One Jabbur whispered in the ear of another, "The Lord taketh and the Lord giveth. Know what? I can't stand the taste of camel meat." And a Jubran stood on a parked camel litter and gave praise to the Lord, saying, "The camel, as you know, is a beast of the desert and we live in the valleys. And Jubrana's only son was ravaged by a camel; we freed him—the pity of it!—from the young beast's jaws in gobbets." Before their minds could even start to deal with these painful memories, the mule appeared. Meekly it looked down on them. Calmly it moved, as though coming from the mansions of the moon. A Jubayra ululated with joy and sprinkled flour on its dignified face. Love shook the J-B-Rs to the core, and they fired off shots and sayings and words of wisdom, and in every mule that arrived they discovered new qualities and benefits: the prophets had depended on the mule in their exhausting journeys to the highest heavens; it had shared with the scholars of Islam their enervating travels across the deserts of Tunisia, Spain, Austria, and Portugal; it had carried books, flagons, and tents for many long eons. We had never heard (the Lord taketh and the Lord giveth) that a camel was capable of crossing a canal; likewise, we had never heard of a camel climbing a mountain. Let us therefore have done with the camel, and that without bothering to mourn or appoint blame—for we were people of the moment. A wounded Jubran yelled that they should fear the Lord and let His creatures speak the word of Truth. Then, with voice raised high, he burst forth, flooding the place with his words, as follows: "Which one among us can forget the Affair of the Oven of Jabrun the Kind? The J-B-Rs are kindly people but this is a true matter. Jabrun the Kind was returning that day mounted on his comfortable young camel, but at the turning by the Great House the camel flew into a rage. It flew into a rage and bashed against the walls and rushed through the streets like a tornado, while Jabrun the Kind, clinging to its back, screamed and the J-B-Rs watched from the doorways and windows and laughed. Then the raging beast managed to throw Jabrun the Kind off its back, only to kick him against the wall, breaking his neck, and then went raging on till it charged into the house of its owner and the walls were brought down on the family of Jabrun the Kind and the camel carried on trampling the place with its legs and its haunches till the oven collapsed and fires broke out. And what then, O wounded Jubran? Even then, the J-B-Rs kept on laughing." At this point, a Jubayr silently rose, rushed over to his camel, and smote it with his weapon as a demonstration of his hatred for such an animal, and the settlement would have turned into one great slaughter were it not for the continued arrival of the mules.

*

The mule found itself at ease in the settlement of the J-B-Rs and applied itself right away to effort and activity, hauling and carrying. Four Jubrans opened a cart-making workshop and helped a hard-working Jabbur to become a smith and an upwardly mobile Jabbur to become a carpenter, and the courtyards, plazas, and compounds turned into places for the assembling of the roofs, wheels, and shafts of carts. The J-B-Rs were delighted when they saw their mules running along the roads pulling the carts behind them to all the neighbouring settlements, and for the first time their own settlement became acquainted with metaled and levelled highways. Experts on the different kinds of trees, wood, and iron and prodigies in the treatment of wounds, the mounting of shoes, and the piercing of mules' abscesses appeared among them, as did households specializing in saddles and stirrups, girthing and harnessing. Theorists undertook to direct the J-B-Rs toward the best ways of treating sores, leg swellings, and back suppurations, and the more the settlement pullulated with mules and carts, the prouder and stouter the J-B-Rs became.

The purity of the mule quickly had its effect on both word and deed. What sort of an age had that been when they had gathered around a jenny and a jack that were trying to mate? What kind of blinding crudeness had it been that allowed them to hurt their eyes with the sight of a she-camel pinned to the ground while her mate foamed and frothed with desire? Let us draw a veil over such memories and be happy for the J-B-Rs as they practice a refined life innocent of mating and groping about in wombs, of birthing and filthy wastes. Purity cast its shade over the whole settlement, and it became calm and biddable, earnest, enterprising, and generous with its wealth. The J-B-R clan became healthy, sound of incisor and molar, and none remained among them whose voice was repulsive like that "most unpleasant of voices," or whose throat produced resounding noise like that of water pouring from a narrow-necked jug. The mule was neither noisy nor disturbing. Its voice was smooth and delicate: neither a bray nor a bleat, but rather a tender delicate sound like a whisper—a mere whisper, incapable of rousing a man from sleep. Indeed, the J-B-Rs began to feel that they had never had a good night's sleep till then. Their throats shrank and their shoulders grew broad. Their noses lengthened and their withers and backsides grew fat. The hauling and carrying, storing, sorting, and trading had also, it seemed, put paid to that certain inherited desire for wife and sons, and it became easy for any J-B-R to go deep into the surrounding settlements for days and months at a time without feeling any anxiety or apprehension. Their sayings, songs, and poetry became free of the abominations of passion and passion-poopers, of betrayal and rapture alike. The vulgarities in which the ages of obscenity had steeped them disappeared from their stories. And very soon, the J-B-Rs had penetrated deep into the calm cocooned world of gravitas, of wisdom, and of sleep innocent of the tumult of dreams.

*

- The voice of the J-B-Rs quivered with sorrow. The Great Jabir, laid out in his winding sheet, indicated to them with a blink of his eyelids that they should sit. One of them whispered through his tears, "Impart to us your last words, Father!" But the Great Jabir continued to stare into the distance in silence.

- One of them hurried to collect sticks in a bundle to remind them that in unity lay strength. But the Great Jabir continued to stare into the distance in silence.

- Quaveringly, the voice of the clan of Jabir rose in a hymn that spoke of a vizier who started life in a pit. But the Great Jabir continued to stare into the distance in silence.

- Someone with a ringing voice chanted the tale of the one who was afflicted in his body by ulcers and whose wife carried him to the ends of the earth in search of a cure. But the Great Jabir continued to stare into the distance in silence.

- Someone with a sweet-toned voice recited the homily of the camel that had crossed the wide open spaces searching for the killer of its friend. But the Great Jabir continued to stare into the distance in silence.

- A melancholy whispering arose, speaking of a truth telling mule that pulled its cart behind it without realizing that the cart had become detached and had fallen into a swamp, taking its owner with it. But the Great Jabir continued to stare into the distance in silence.

- The face of the J-B-Rs leaped from the corners to the ceiling, to the bedding, and finally to the face of the Great Jabir, which radiated light: "Impart to us your last words, Father!"

- And before the Great Jabir's eyelashes closed, he whispered forcefully, "My final counsel to you is, 'Get a pig!'"

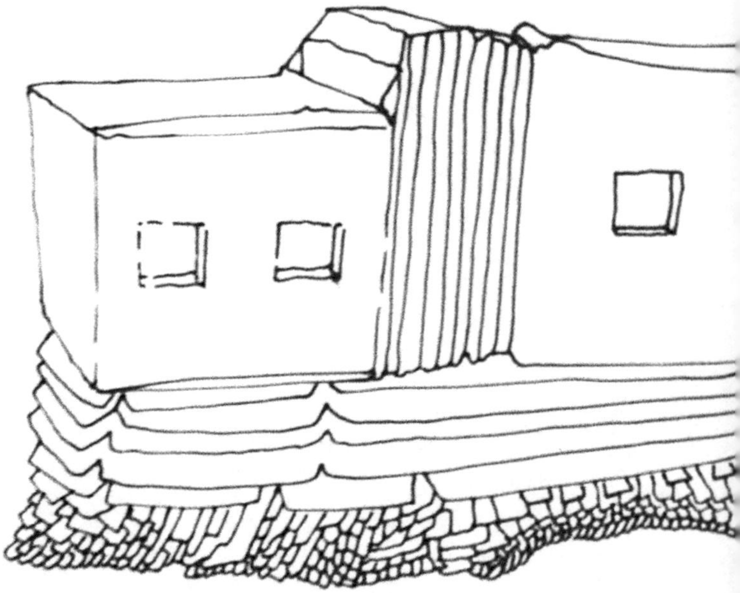

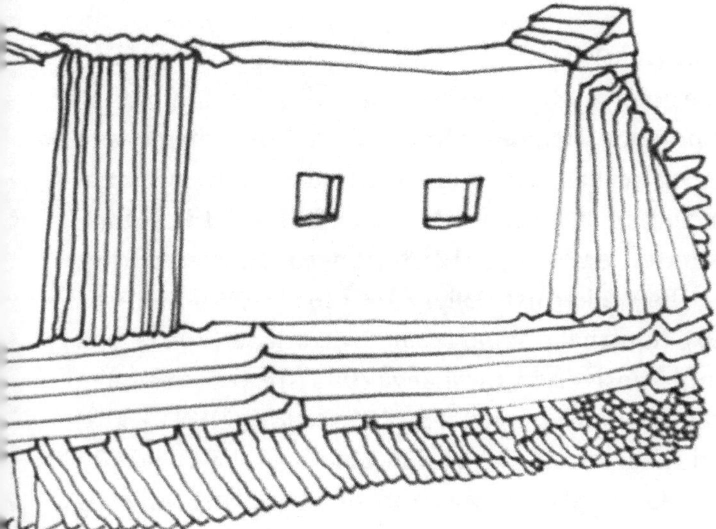

Wael Shawky (b. 1971)
Born in Alexandria, Egypt, where he still lives and works, Shawky's practice includes film, installation, drawing and performance. He has held numerous solo shows internationally, including at Hammer Museum, USA (2013), Kunst-Werke Institute, Germany (2012), Nottingham Contemporary, UK (2011), the Walker Art Gallery, UK (2011), Citta Dell'Arte, Italy (2010), Kunsthalle Winterthur, Switzerland (2007), and Ludwigsburg Kunstverein, Germany (2005). He has presented work at the Sharjah Biennial 11 (2013), dOCUMENTA (13) (2012) and the Istanbul Biennial in 2005 and the Venice Biennale in 2003. In 2011 he was awarded the Ernst Schering Foundation Art Award and in 2012 he was the joint winner of the Abraaj Group Art Prize. In addition to his work as an artist, Wael Shawky runs MASS Alexandria, the first Independent Studio Study Program for young artists in Alexandria, Egypt. In 2011, he undertook residencies at Sharjah Art Foundation as part of their Witness Programme and with the Serpentine's Edgware Road Project, which was organised in collaboration with the Townhouse Gallery, Cairo and the Delfina Foundation, London.

Mohamed Mustagab (1938-2005)
Born in the town of Dayrut in Upper Egypt, Mustagab received little formal education but secured a position at the Academy of the Arabic Language in Cairo and later became general director. He published his first short story *The 11th Commandment* in al-Hilal magazine in 1969. His short novel *The Secret History of Numan Abd al-Hafiz* (1983) won the Egyptian State Incentive Prize in 1984 and was selected as one of the top hundred Arabic novels of the twentieth century. It is also included in the collection of short stories *Tales from Dayrut* (1984) alongside the three stories in this book, which was translated into English and published by the American University of Cairo in 2008.

We would like to thank the following people, whose contribution to this book and to the exhibitions has been invaluable: Mohamed Mustagab, who has kindly given permission to reprint the three of his father's stories that inspired the *Al Araba Al Madfuna* films; Wiener Festwochen for their support in the production of *Al Araba Al Madfuna II*, Andrée Sfeir-Semler and Anna Nowak at Sfeir-Semler Gallery; Nicholas Logsdail and Greg Hilty at Lisson Gallery; Susanne Pfeffer, Director and Nina Tabassomi, Curator at the Fridericianum, Kassel; Neil Hewison, Associate Director for Editorial Programs, Yasmine Gado, Rights & Contracts Manager and Soha Mohsen at the American University in Cairo; Reem Shadid, Deputy Director at Sharjah Art Foundation and the wider team at Sharjah Art Foundation; Jochen Volz, Head of Programmes, Rebecca Lewin, Exhibition Curator, Mike Gaughan, Gallery Manager and the wider team at the Serpentine Galleries; Hani Charaf; Karen Marta, Dustin Cosentino and Quinn Lewington of Karen Marta Editorial Consulting.

Julia Peyton-Jones
Director, Serpentine Galleries and Co-Director, Exhibitions and Programmes

Hans Ulrich Obrist
Co-director of Exhibitions and Programmes and Director of International Projects

Hoor Al-Qasimi
President, Sharjah Art Foundation

Horsemen Adore Perfumes and other stories

Wael Shawky

Editor
Karen Marta
Editorial Coordinators
Jochen Volz, Reem Shadid, Rebecca Lewin
Design
Hani Charaf
English Copyeditor
Mary Lehner
Translation
Nasser Wanous
Arabic Copyeditor
Noor Ismail
Editorial Assistant
Quinn Lewington

Printed in Ajman by Nabeel Printing Press

All artwork by Wael Shawky, 2013

Quote on p.7 taken from Mohamed Mustagab, *The J-B-Rs*

Al Araba Al Madfuna II is co-produced by

Wiener Festwochen

ISBN 978-1-908617-17-0
Serpentine Galleries
ISBN 978-9948-444-81-7
Sharjah Art Foundation
ISBN 978-3-86335-487-9
Koenig Books

Published by:

Sharjah Art Foundation
Arts Area
PO Box 19989, Sharjah
United Arab Emirates
www.sharjahart.org

Serpentine Galleries
Kensington Gardens
London W2 3XA
t +44 (0)20 7402 6075
f +44 (0)20 7402 4103
www.serpentinegalleries.org

Koenig Books Ltd
at the Serpentine Gallery
Kensington Gardens
London W2 3XA
www.koenigbooks.co.uk

Distributed by:

Europe
Buchhandlung Walther König, Köln
Ehrenstr. 4, 50672 Köln
T: +49 (0) 221 / 20 59 6-53
F: +49 (0) 221 / 20 59 6-60
verlag@buchhandlung-walther-koenig.de

UK & Eire
Cornerhouse Publications
70 Oxford Street
GB-Manchester M1 5NH
T: +44 (0) 161 200 15 03
F: +44 (0) 161 200 15 04
publications@cornerhouse.org

UAE
Sharjah Art Foundation
Arts Area
PO Box 19989, Sharjah
United Arab Emirates
www.sharjahart.org

Americas
ARTBOOK | D.A.P.
155 Sixth Avenue, 2nd Floor
New York, NY 10013
T: +1 212-627-1999
F: +1 212-627-9484
orders@dapinc.com
www.artbook.com

وائل شوقي

Koenig Books

الفرسان يعشقون الطيور
وحكايات أخرى

SHARJAH ART FOUNDATION

SERPENTINE
GALLERIES

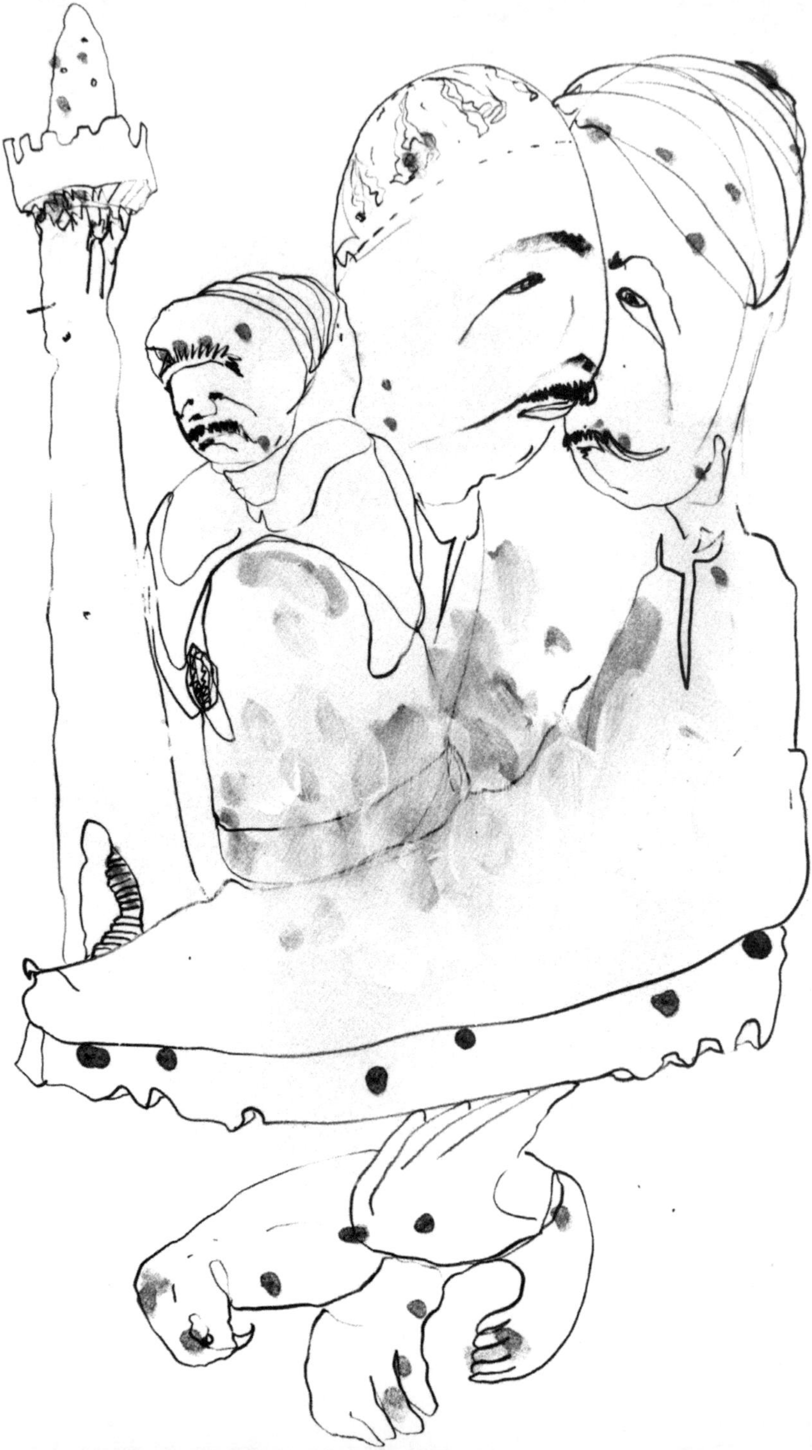

"أوصنا يا أبانا."
فظل جابر الكبير ممعناً وصامتاً.

محمد مستجاب

المحتويات

المقدمة

جوليا بيتون جونز
هانس أولريخ أوبريست

إصدار هذا الكتاب تم بالتعاون بين مؤسسة الشارقة للفنون وغاليريهات سيربنتاين بمناسبة افتتاح معارض وائل شوقي، في غاليري سيربنتاين، لندن في عام ٢٠١٣، وفي الشارقة في عام ٢٠١٤. إن هذا التركيز الرائع على أعمال شوقي لم يكن ليكون ممكناً لولا التعاون القائم بين المؤسستين وعلاقتنا مع الفنان التي تطورت على مدى سنوات عديدة وبأشكال متعددة. فقد شارك شوقي في معارض جماعية كـ معرض "على طريق إدجوار" في غاليري سيربنتاين في عام ٢٠١٢، وبينالي الشارقة الحادي عشر في ٢٠١٣، وفي معرض "اغتراب مرة ثانية" الذي شاركت مؤسسة الشارقة للفنون في إنتاجه عام ٢٠٠٩، وفي ٢٠١١ تمت دعوته من قبل المؤسستين للإقامة في مقرهما الخاص.

آخر أفلام وائل شوقي العرابة المدفونة الثاني (٢٠١٣) يعرض للمرة الأولى في كل من المملكة المتحدة والشارقة. حيث أنتج بالتعاون ما بين مؤسسة الشارقة للفنون وفينر فيستوشين، والذي سيكون على رأس قائمة المعارض التي تقيمها المؤسستين. هذا العمل الجميل والمثير للتفكير هو حصيلة الكثير من الموضوعات التي تناولها الفنان على مدى ممارسته الفنية وهو الثاني في سلسلة

أفلامه التي استلهمها من الكاتب المصري محمد مستجاب. تطرح هذه الأفلام (العرابة المدفونة ٢٠١٢، والعرابة المدفونة الثاني) كتابات مستجاب لجمهور عالمي أوسع، كما نأمل بأن تقدم للقراء فهماً أعمق لمدى أهمية السرد ومصادره التي وظفها شوقي في أفلامه ورسوماته وأعماله التركيبية.

سلسلة أفلامه السابقة كباريه الحروب الصليبية ستعرض بجانب أعماله الجديدة في غاليري سيربنتاين، هذا الفيلم التحريكي يعتمد على وثائق تاريخية ووقائع ملموسة مصدرها كتاب المؤلف اللبناني أمين معلوف "الحرب الصليبية كما رآها العرب" ويحاول التساؤل عن الدوافع الاجتماعية والاقتصادية وراء هذه "الحروب المقدسة". إن للقصص التي لها علاقة بتاريخ وثقافة مصر وطن شوقي الأصلي وبالشرق الأوسط على نحو أوسع جرى إعادة سردها وتمثيلها. لكن في الفيلم الجديد لاعبو الأدوار هم من الأطفال بدلاً من الدمى، أصواتهم المدبلجة وشواربهم الاصطناعية تشير إلى نية وائل شوقي جعل المشاهد يسأل عن درجة الالتزام التي يتوجب علينا الوصول إليها من أجل استقبال الحكمة. وإلى جانب رسوماته هناك سلسلة جديدة يسعدنا إدراجها في هذا الكتاب كتوضيحات أنتجت خصيصاً لهذا المشروع، الدمى التي ينتجها وائل شوقي والأعمال التركيبية تخلق عوالم سريالية، وأماكن تتداخل فيها الحقيقة والأسطورة والتجارب الحية.

ينوّع شوقي ممارسته الفنية على نحو لا يصدق، فممارسته للفن تشمل فن الأداء والسينما والتجهيزات في الفراغ، والملاحظات النقدية العميقة والمتصلة فيما بينها بشأن التقاليد العربية والثقافة المرتبطة على نحو كبير بمشاهدينا الخاصين، وهو لقي ترحيباً دولياً يستحقه لالتزامه المتكرر بعمليات سرد القصص وبنتائجها وسط المجتمعات المحلية والعالمية على حد سواء. وعندما سألنا شوقي عن مدى اهتمامه بكتب التاريخ والقصص، أخبرنا: "أنا مفتون بالفكرة التي تقتضي ترجمة التاريخ. لا أؤمن بالتاريخ إلى ذاك الحد... وأنا لا أنص على أن هناك حقيقة أو كذب. إنما مجرد طريقة مختلفة لرؤية الأمور." إنه ذاك العنصر ذاته

في أعماله الذي يشكل المحور للمعارض ولهذا الكتاب، والذي يستمد شكله من الأعراف الأدبية العربية والإنجليزية على حد سواء. بالإضافة إلى القصص الثلاث القصيرة التي استلهمها شوقي في فيلميه العرابة المدفونة، يتضمن هذا المنشور مقدمة متمعنة كتبتها حور القاسمي رئيس مؤسسة الشارقة للفنون تعرف فيها القارئ على استخدام شوقي للسرد القصصي؛ ومفهوم هذا التقليد في الشرق الأوسط. ونحن مدينون لهذا الالتزام والتفاني.

جوليا بيتون جونز
مدير، غاليرهات سيربنتاين، ومدير مشارك للمعارض والبرامج

هانس أولريخ أوبريست
مدير مشارك للمعارض والبرامج ومدير المشروعات الدولية

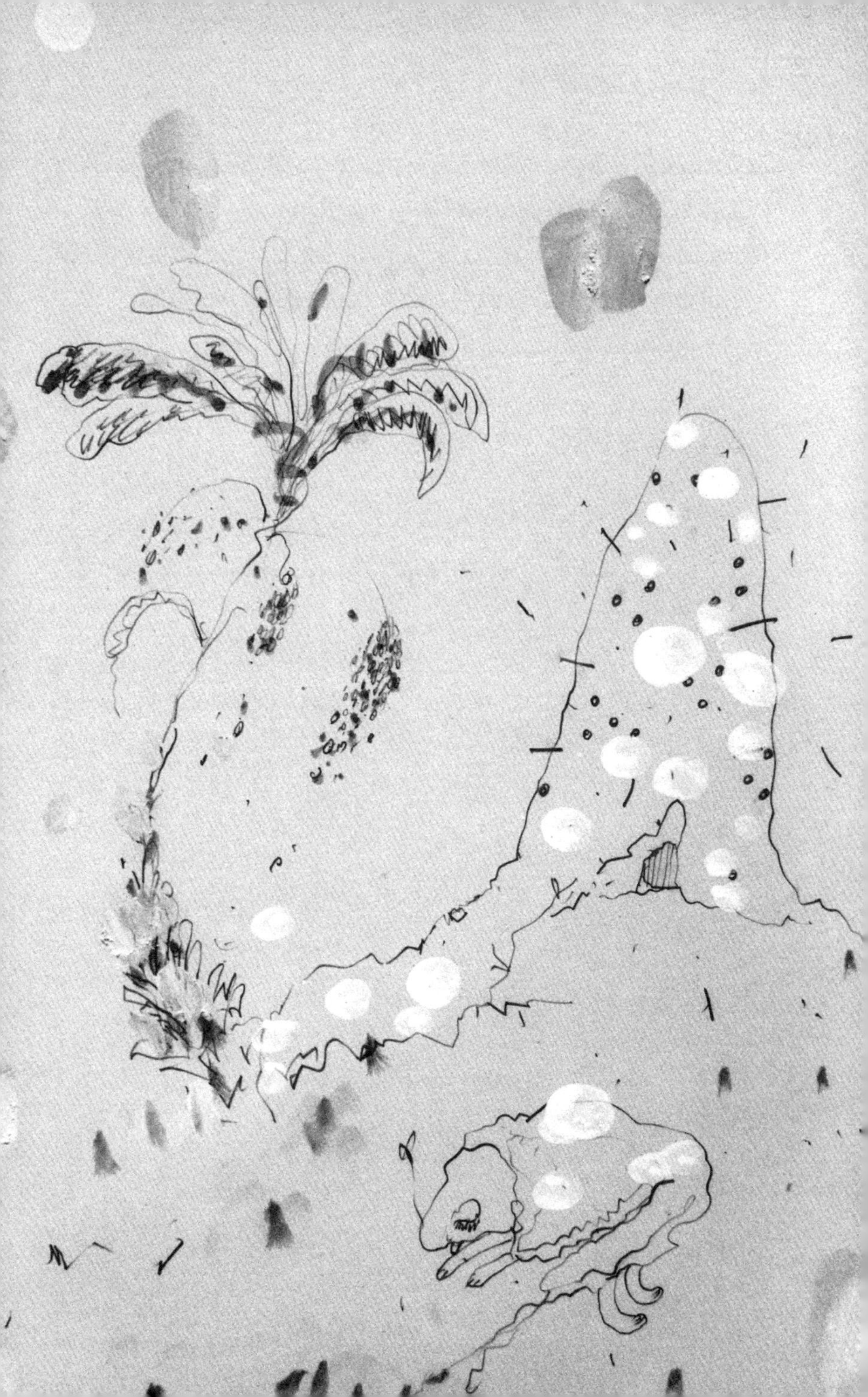

يتلو/ يروي

حور القاسمي

نظراً للنشأة ضمن عائلة عربية ولأن الأب مؤرخ وكاتب، فإننا غالباً ما نسمع الكثير من القصص. قصص من طفولة والدي، وقصص تاريخية وحكايات وأساطير قديمة، كثيراً ما يستخدمها والدي كمراجع لهذه القصص التي يكتبها كسيناريوهات وكتب. كما أن حكاية القصص تحتل جزءاً كبيراً من الثقافة العربية، إنها تقليد متوارث في الكثير من الثقافات وتستخدم منذ زمن بعيد كطريقة لغرس القيم الأخلاقية وتعليم التاريخ وحفظه وغالباً ما استخدمت أثناء الممارسات الدينية. وبناء على القيم، تم تمرير القصص التي حفظت عن ظهر قلب من جيل إلى جيل لتشكيل أساس لمجتمع وإيصال رسالة وحدة الوظائف الروحية والشعائرية، وحالما تصل الرسالة تنتهي الرسالة عادة. ومع عملية سرد الحكاية وتكرارها، يمكن لقصص مختلفة أن تنشأ من جديد أو تتغير، مظهرة نتائج مختلفة بالنسبة لأفعال شخص ما. في التقاليد الشفوية تبقى القصص حية عبر تكرارها المرة تلوى الأخرى، وخلال هذه العملية تخضع تفاصيلها لتغيرات وتعديلات عديدة بطبيعة الحال. وعند التفكير بالمؤلف تميل القصص للظهور بوصفها من عمل الأفراد بدل أن تكون نتاج جهد جماعي. لكن في معظم أفلام وائل شوقي

يكون الممثلون متجمعين وفق جاليات ومجتمعات، وكنتيجة فإن المسألة لها علاقة بالمؤلف. إن الأوضاع المستخدمة كمنهج لتعليم الأخلاقيات والقيم والمعايير الثقافية والاختلافات عادة ما تحدث في بيئات اجتماعية حقيقية تقدم أمثلة عن الكيفية المطبقة بها المعرفة وعن تقديم أداة لنقل المعرفة في سياق اجتماعي. وكما نرى في "العرابة المدفونة" يقوم الأولاد بأدوار سرد القصة، في هذه الحالة، ليس فقط المستمع هو من يتعلم، وإنما الراوي الذي يصبح أيضاً مدركاً لفهمه الخاص وللظروف المحيطة. هذه العملية من حكاية القصص هي عملية تخويل طالما أن الراوي ينقل على نحو مؤثر الأفكار، مع الممارسة، فهو يتمكن من إظهار مكمن الإنجاز البشري. وتنفتح القصة على المعرفة الموجودة وتقيم جسوراً لإيجاد حل.

هذه الأشكال المختلفة من سرد القصص وإعادة حكايتها واضحة للعيان في عمل وائل شوقي حيث يستخدم الأدب العربي إلى جانب لحظات في التاريخ كمصادر للإلهام ومسائل الموضوع في أفلامه. في الحلقتين الأولى والثانية من "العرابة المدفونة" ينظر شوقي إلى القصص القصيرة للروائي المصري محمد مستجاب (١٩٣٨–٢٠٠٥) كمصدر رئيسي للحكايات من أجل سلسلة أفلامه. وعندما سئل "لماذا مستجاب" قال إنه يفكر في طرق العمل مع قصص مستجاب منذ خمسة عشر عاماً. "إنه معني بالطريقة التي يسرد فيها مستجاب الأحداث التاريخية؛ مازجاً بين الدين والحياة لخلق قصص تبدو قابلة للتصديق لكنك تعرف أنها أسطورية. يصف شوقي لغة مستجاب بأنها "رابط بين الميتافيزيائيات والفيزيائيات"، وهو معني بالناس الذين يطبقون الممارسات الخارقة للطبيعة، مثل السحر أو القرآن الكريم من أجل الكسب المادي".

في هذه الاستعادة للماضي والتأمل فيه، يؤفلم وائل قصة بينما يتم سرد قصة أخرى، وبالتالي أنت تشاهد قصة لكنك تسمع قصة أخرى. إنه يحاول القول أن لديك نظامان يعملان بالتوازي كل من أجل الآخر، أو أن لديك أطفالاً يتحدثون بأصوات الكبار أو أنك تسمع قصة واحدة وترى أخرى يتم تمثيل أحداثها أمامك. في كلا الفيلمين العرابة المدفونة الأول والعرابة المدفونة الثاني، استندت الأوضاع

والقصص التي تمت أفلمتها على تجارب شوقي في هذه القرى في صعيد مصر وعلى القصص التي سمعها عندما كان هناك.

يروي العرابة المدفونة حكاية الجبارنة لمحمد مستجاب. وهو يظهر اجتماع قبيلة تدعى الجبارنة بانتظار الوصية الأخيرة لجابر الكبير وهو يحتضر، حيث سينفذون تلك الوصية دونما أدنى شك. تدور الأحداث في قرية تقع بالقرب من موقع يجري التنقيب فيه عن الآثار قرب معبد أوسيرون في مدينة أبيدوس القديمة. ارتدى الأطفال ثياب الرجال وهم متجمعون في مكان تحت الأرض ويتحدثون بأصوات الرجال. بالقرب من معبد أبيدوس، يقضي سكان هذه القرية سنوات في البحث عن كنز، يحفرون على أمل إيجاد أنفاق تقود إلى الغرف الفرعونية. نرى أحدهم وهو يحفر في وسط الغرفة بينما يجتمع الآخرون لحكاية الحكاية. تعاد القصة باستبدال الحيوان إلى أن تنتهي عندما يطلب منهم الحصول على خنزير، وهو الحيوان المحرم أكل لحمه في الإسلام، أية معضلة هذه إذا لم يتمكنوا من العيش مع الخنازير كما يعيشون مع الحمير أو يأكلون لحمها مثلما فعلوا مع الجمال، هل سيفعلوا مع الخنازير في نهاية الأمر مثلما فعلوا مع الجمال حيث عاشوا معها ومن ثم أكلوا لحمها؟

تتضمن مثل هذه العناصر الفكرة الجوهرية للبنية السردية ببدايات وأوساط ونهايات يمكن التعرف عليها. مع ذلك، ومع هذه النهاية المفاجئة ومع الافتراض الآلي للمشاهد باستمرارية القصة وتكرار الأفعال نفسها الآن مع الخنزير، لا تنتهي القصة على نحو مؤكد، ويبدو على الجبارنة أنهم عَلِقوا في براثن عملية لانهائية وتكرارية تنتهي كل مرة بالفشل وخيبة الأمل والأسى.

في فيلم العرابة المدفونة الثاني يستخدم شوقي قصتين لمحمد مستجاب، هما القربان و الفرسان يعشقون العطور. في الفرسان يعشقون العطور يستخدم مستجاب هذا التكرار حيث قصة الساحرة الجميلة التي يكرهها القرويون بسبب ما تقوم به من "الامتصاص الدموي لأرزاق الفقراء" ويدعون الفارس للثأر منها والتباحث في الأمر، وبدلاً من الحل ينتهي بها الأمر بالزواج من الفارس والذي

يحتفل به القرويون، وبعد أربعة أيام تخرج من قصرها ساحبة خلفها جسد الفارس المضمخ بالعطور وتقطع رأسه. هذا السيناريو للأحداث يتكرر عدداً من المرات عبر القصة مع فرسان مختلفين.

في كلا الفيلمين يتحدث الأطفال بالعربية الفصحى، التي نادراً ما يتم الحديث بها في المجالس والأحوال الاجتماعية، لكن بدلاً من ذلك يظهر هذا الاستخدام للغة الفصحى بوصفه صوتاً للسلطة والتقاليد، المستخدم في الأدب والتعليم، لغة القرآن الكريم، وعند كتابة الأخبار. لا يفهم الأطفال بالضرورة ماذا يتلون لكنهم يمتلكون الصوت الشبيه بصوت الراوي، ويمكن لهذا أن يبدو كصوت للسلطة، ويمكن أن يشير أو يستحضر نوعاً من الصدقية التي تعالج القضايا التي يناقشونها. يستخدم شوقي في عمله الأطفال والدمى كممثلين في أفلامه، الأطفال لا يتحرجون وبالتالي فإن أدائهم أكثر عفوية وأقل تكلفاً، وبالتالي تصبح الشخصيات التي يمثلونها واقعية وقابلة للتصديق. يبدو أن استخدام شوقي لهذه المقاربة الكونية لرواية القصص هو لتجسير الهوة الثقافية بين الأجيال (والمتعلقة بالأعمار)، متخلياً عن فكرة التمييز على أساس العمر.

تشير أعمال شوقي أيضاً إلى لحظات في التاريخ، مشار إليها من خلال عيون الأطفال أو عبر إعادة إحيائهم للأحداث، أو من خلال الدمى المتحركة، المنفصلة عن هذا التاريخ الذي تقوم هذه الدمى بتمثيل أدواره دون مبالغة وبكل براءة. ويمكن لهذا أن يجعل القصة أكثر عمومية أو كونية وأيضاً، وفق شوقي، أكثر قابلية للتصديق.

في سلسلة أفلام شوقي كبريه الحروب الصليبية، تقوم الدمى بإعادة إحياء تاريخ الحروب الصليبية، عبر استلهام كتاب أمين معلوف الحروب الصليبية كما رآها العرب. ومن حين لآخر يخلق شوقي أحداثاً مزيفة حيث يقوم بتوثيقها كما هو الحال في سلسلة تيليماتش، كما أنه يعدّل هذه اللحظات في التاريخ. في عمله غالباً ما ينظر شوقي إلى التغيرات السياسية والاجتماعية في مصر بدءاً من جمال عبد الناصر إلى أنور السادات انتهاء بحسني مبارك. غالباً ما يستخدم المناظر

الطبيعية لوصف هذه التغيرات، مستخدماً المواقع الزراعية الفلاحية التي تمثل مصادر معيشة المصرين التي تجلب إلى المتاجر الكبرى، كما تمثل حالة التهجين بين التحديث وهذا المجتمع البدوي–القبلي. أثناء مناقشة مع شوقي أشار إلى محاولته التقاط نظام ما في حالة الانتقال أو مجتمع أثناء مرحلة انتقالية. وهذه الفكرة يمكن مشاهدتها في أعمال مثل المربع الاسفلتي، حيث يربط مصر بمجتمع زراعي ويربط الصحراء الجافة مع مجتمع عربي. فهو يتحدث عن ثقافة جافة من حيث المنظر الطبيعي لكن أيضاً من حيث الثقافة نفسها، وهو نشأ عندما كان طفلاً في مكة المكرمة، وهو يقول إنه كان دائماً يشعر أن المنظر الطبيعي في مصر كان أكثر أنوثة وفي المملكة العربية السعودية أكثر رجولة، الزراعة والثقافة الرطبة في مصر والثقافة الجافة في الخليج.

إن شوقي معني بالطريقة التي نكتب بها التاريخ، وبتوثيقه وتفسيره، وذلك عبر التمكن من ترجمة كتاب إلى شكل بصري. فأنت غالباً ما تُترك في حالة من التساؤل بشأن هوية المؤلف، ورؤاه السياسية، والسياق التاريخي، والدين، والأقلية العرقية، وعلم النفس، أو الخصائص الشخصية أو السيرة الحياتية – لاستخلاص المعنى من عمل المؤلف. وبخلاف عمله الكهف أو الأعمال التي يقرأ فيها مقاطع من القرآن الكريم، نكتشف معنى "لاهوتياً"، "رسالة" اَعز وجل". سألت شوقي عن السبب الذي جعل الدين يحتل مكانة بالغة الأهمية في عمله، فأجاب أن ذلك كان جزءاً من طفولته، فقد عاش في مكة المكرمة، وكان متأثراً جداً بقوة اللغة وبدأ بقراءة الصوفية، وكان مفتوناً بقوة الكلمة واللغة وقال إنه "حتى لو لم أكن أؤمن بالتاريخ فإنني أحاول استخدام مصدر التاريخ المكتوب لتحليل التاريخ. انتقاد التاريخ من خلال الحفاظ على الدقة العالية باستخدام العبارة الدقيقة من مثل كلمات أسامة بن منقذ في كباريه الحروب الصليبية: الطريق إلى القاهرة".

جميع الأقوال مأخوذة من حوار بين وائل شوقي والكاتب في أكتوبر ٢٠١٣.

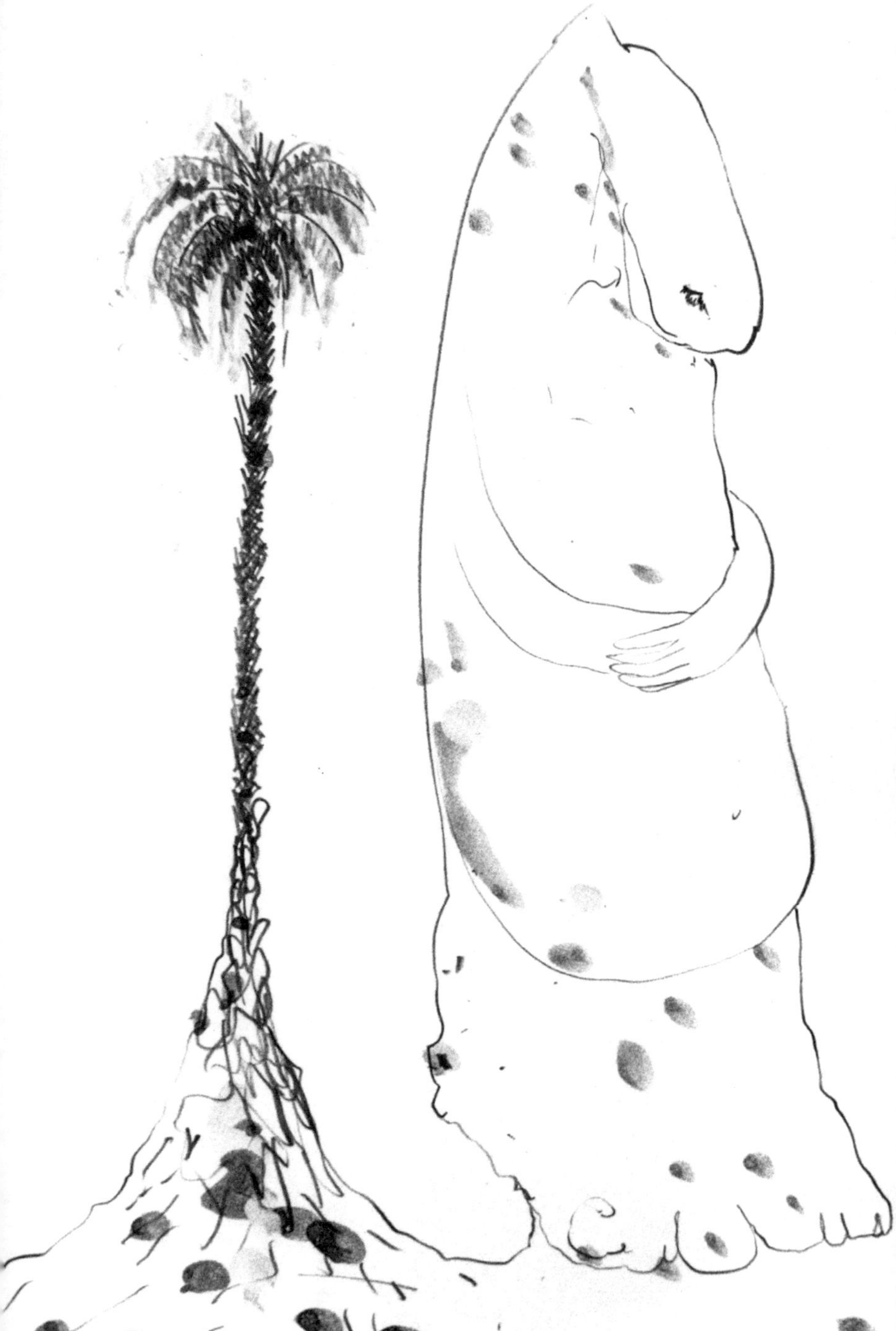

الفرسان يعشقون الطيور
وحكايات أخرى

محمد مستجاب

القربان

محمد مستجاب

لا نعرف بالتحديد متى حدث ذلك لكنه بالتأكيد حدث، ورد ذكره على لسان أبي ولم تنكره أمي، وثرثر فيه يحيى حقي ويوسف إدريس وخليل عيسى الغار وعلي الجهيني والخواجة بسادة والمقدس بباوي وعبد الودود الأخنف، وعبد الودود الأخنف كان أكثر القوم إلحاحاً في تأكيد حدوثه، ويوسف إدريس حاول مستميتاً أن يحدد زمان حدوثه وتجرأ ذات مرة وقال إن ما حدث حدث منذ زمان طويل، وعلى وجه الدقة أيام الكوارث التي اجتاحت سدوم وعمورية، على أننا في عصرنا القائم لا نملك دليلاً محدداً يمكن لنا أن نقف على مادته لتحديد ذلك الوقت، لو أن الشيخ علي فقيه القرية المتبحر لا يزال على قيد الحياة لكان منحنا ما نستند عليه، فقد كان الشيخ علي يملك كتاباً أصفر مطلسماً، قيل إن القرية ظلت تتوارثه سراً حتى انتهى الأمر بالكتاب إليه، وقيل إن الشيخ مات بسبب محاولته فك الطلاسم الحاوية كل ما نبغيه من تفاصيل، ثم قيل وما أكثر ما قيل إن قرينة الشيخ الشهير قد اصطحبت كتاب القرية الطلسم مهاجرة له قريتها تلك الواقعة خلف الجبل الأزرق في المكان الذي تغيب فيه الشمس، ولا أنكر معظم ما اختلف عليه قومي كان زمن الحادث أو بدايته أو

مكانه، البعض يعتقد أن قبلي البلد مكان مناسب للبداية حيث جامع الأمير سنان وقبره وشاهده، وآخرون يعتقدون أن بحري البلد أكثر تناسباً للبداية، فهناك كنيسة الأنبا سرابامون وقبره وشاهده، وفريق ثالث ومعظمه من سلالات غريبة عن البلدة يؤكد أن ما حدث بدأ في الوسط حيث تكثر البيوت السرية، ومنازل البغاء وتجمعات الراقصات وجوقات الغوازي، لكن واحداً من قبلي أو بحري أو وسط البلد حقيقة لم يحاول أن يشك في الحدث ذاته.

— ١ —

والحدث ذاته بدأ في ظهر نهار جمعة (في رواية عبد الودود الأخنف)، وفي صباح يوم سبت النور (في رواية المقدس بباوي)، كان أحد رجال قريتي جالساً على رأس حقله يردد مواويل الصبر الشهيرة حينما ثقل لسانه وتلجلج فارتبك الرجل وفزع، لم يخرس تماماً لكنه فقد سيولة الكلمات المتدفقة من حنجرته، تهتكت كلماته في قاع الحلق ثم خرجت مطحونة مجرد حروف لا يربط السابق فيها باللاحق إلا تهتهة عواء ممطوط متوتر، وظل الرجل في مكانه وحيداً يحاول معاجلة إخراج الكلام من حلقه، تعاونت الشفتان واللسان وقاع الحلق وعضلات جوف الخدود وسقف الخشم كي تربط الحروف وتصحح الكلمات وتنظم ترتيب الجزيئات وتغلي الأوشاب الصوتية، لكن محاولة الرجل فشلت.

وهرع الرجل إلى داره متأبطاً رعبه، ليس متأبطاً فقط رعبه بل وقاضماً لقمة كبيرة من الرعب تتخبط في فمه وتدفع بالصفرة والفزع والوجل إلى كل كيانه، وهرعت قريتي إلى رجلها تقف بجواره، من حضر ليفتح الكتاب ويفك (العمل)، ومن جاء ليفصد الدماغ وما بين الكتفين، ومن أتى ليأخذ قطعة من ملابس المصاب ليحرقها كي تخطو عليها زوجه العاقر سبع خطوات ثم تستحم

في ليلة مقمرة بماء مذبوحة فيه ضفدعة، ومن قدم ليفسر الحدث كله ويعلقه في رقبة الكفر الذي انتهك حياة المصاب وجعله يتخلى عن دينه فلا يزور مشاهد القديسين، وقريتي لئيمة، تنفعل وتصرخ وتواسي وتفتي، ثم تترك الأمر في نهاية الأمر لصاحب الأمر، حيث تعود إلى خدورها مقتنعة أن ما حدث واجب الحدوث، فلا بد بين الحين والحين من واحد يلدغ بعقرب أو يغرق في النهر أو يسقط عليه حائط أو يهوى من فوق نخلة أو يخرج له عفريت هواش الشهير ليرعبه ويشله، أو تناوره عبدة السواقي لتجرفه معها إلى بطن ساقية أو جوف هويس نعم: قريتي لئيمة وتعلم جيداً أنها بين وقت وآخر لا بد أن تستقبل حادثاً كهذا، نسبة قدرية محددة من رجالها تقدمها قرباناً للزمن، ليحمد ا َبعد ذلك كل من لم يكن مصاباً.

وكادت قريتي تنتهي من فلسفة الحادث تمهيدًا لأن تضع ذراعها تحت رأسها وتنام، لكن الأمر لم يتوقف عند مجرد واحد يخرس، ففي نهاية ذاك اليوم فقد تاجر حمير النطق دون أن يخرج من داره ليواجه عفريت هواش أوعبدة السواقي. وقبل أن تفيق البلد من وجلها خرست امرأة متدينة، وفي شرق البلد نهش ثعبان لسان المشرف على الأسواق، وانشرخ لسان صانع تماثيل، خمسة، ستة، ستون، مائة، كل القرية، حتى خطيب مسجدها الورع، الأبيض كالحليب، الطيب كنبي، المؤدب كبنت بنوت، الشهم كفارس، الشجاع كابن أبي طالب، هذا الخطيب المفوه انفتح فمه عن آخره وهو واقف على المنبر يحث المؤمنين على الصبر ونبذ المعصية والتعلق بحبال الخالق، وظل فمه مفتوحاً حتى تنبهت إليه الجماهير، فهرعوا إليه وحملوه في جو مذعور مرعوب مليء بالمواء والنقنقة والانزعاج، لا بد من الاستعاذة با َولا بد من مصمصة الشفاه لكن قريتي خرست، إنشل لسانها وذابت حراشيفه وفشل في صنع أي حرف من تلك الحروف العظيمة التي تكون الكلام، خرست وأصاب الذعر جسدها والدوار رأسها، وانفتحت عيونها رعباً، أصابها الداء فظلت تجري يميناً ويساراً، وتلج بيوت القديسين ومشاهد المشايخ وأنصار اَ، تدق الخردل والحلبة والدمسيسة

وحلف البر والخلنجان وتصنع منه مزيداً تشربه على ريق النوم، تعرج إلى المقابر فتسف التراب ثم تنزل إلى بطون الترع ومسارب المياه تستحم أو تدهن جسدها بالوحل، تتوسل إلى الرب في المذابح على ضوء الشموع ثم تؤدي صباح كل يوم ركعتي صلاة الخوف، تقطع جريد النخل وتصنع منه صلباناً وتنام تحتها في الليالي المقمرة ثم تنقض الصلبان وتهرع إلى باحة المسجد لتبكي وتندب وتستصرخ الواحد القهار، تناوش داءها الرهيب أو يناوشها الداء الرهيب فلا تعود إلى نفسها إلا والمستحيل الأبكم متقوقع داخل خشمها، عاجزة أن تجمع الحرف جنب الحرف أو ترص الكلمة وراء الكلمة لتفشل في آخر النهار في تكوين جملة، أو تنجح في حالات نادرة أن ترص الحرف جنب الحرف والكلمة وراء الكلمة لتكتشف في آخر النهار أن الجملة التي وصلت إليها ليست الجملة المقصودة، كلام مبتور مفتت مهشم ممزق يتسرب من أفواه واسعة يطن داخلها لسان من اللحم الطري البارد الراقد وسط بحيرة لعاب.

—٢—

محاولات شاقة تلك التي بذلوها لكي يصلوا إلى سر النكبة وتعليل المصيبة، لجأوا إلى بعض ذوي الدراية والخوارق في المناطق المجاورة وذبحوا لهم الخرفان والديوك الرومية، وعانوا من بلع الأحجبة أو مضغها، وعانوا من القفز فوق الحفر الدائرية المملوءة بالنار المعبق بالبخور وذيول الفيران وأرجل الزواحف، ثم استعانوا بمن يمر بهم من الغجر والأعراب، وامتلأت القرية بالدجالين والسحرة وأصحاب الرؤية ومعاشري الشياطين، فلما ظلت المحنة قائمة سافرت وفود منهم إلى كردفان وسيوه ووادي المساخيط، وكل واحد له تفسير وتبرير، فتوى من الواحات تقول إن واحداً من أهل القرية لا بد قد قارف سوءاً مع أمه أو أبيه، ومقولة أخرى أن واحداً من أهل القرية لا بد قد مارس العيب على أجولة الدقيق فغضب (النعمة) على البلد.

وربما كانت آخر محاولات حل الرصد المعمول للقرية، أن أشير لها أن تقوم بذبح طفل يتيم أحمر الشعر، وأن يلطخوا بدمه آليات ومؤخرات الرجال وبطن أفخاذ النساء، فلما قامت البلد بتحضير العلاج على طفل اختلسوه من نجع مجاور، ولما افتقد النجع المجاور طفله اليتيم أحمر الشعر، وبعد أن نمى إلى علمهم أنه تحول إلى عقار لشقاء البلد من الخرس، قامت النجوع الحانقة بمحاصرة البلدة، ثم اقتحموها وذبحوا أبناء لها ورجالاً وسبوا ثماني نساء، وبالوا على وجه مائة شيخ من أعيانها، لتتوقف قريتي بعدها عن تجريب أي حل آخر، ظل الذعر كابساً على صدر قريتي صامتاً وحشياً وعراً، صحيح أن الحقول جفت واجتاحها الفقر والصفرة، وصحيح أن بياض البيوت تهشم وسقطت القوالب من أصداغ الأبواب، وصحيح أن حيواناتها أجهضت وذوت، وصحيح أن التراب عفر الوجوه واللحى والعمائم لكن ذلك كله لم يكن يهم قريتي، الذي يهمها هو لسانها فلم تكن البلد مرتبطة نهائياً بالعمل اليدوي، هي في مجال آخر؛ قرية متاجرة كل كبارها ورجالات أعيانها تجار، تجار عجول وجواميس وفراخ وردة ونخالة وعسل وحبوب وخضراوات؛ يعتمدون أول ما يعتمدون على تلك العضلة الكنز؛ اللسان، بلسانهم يجاملون ويجادلون ويستدرجون ويقسمون بالحي القيوم والكتب المقدسة ويمدحون ويكذبون ويغتابون ويدفعون ويدافعون ويسامرون، لسان مرن متحرك يظل يلعب داخل الفم ثم يفرز في الوقت المناسب الجملة المناسبة، يهمس بأرق وأنضر وأجمل الكلمات، ويفح بألعن وأقسى الكلام يشم ويتذوق هذا اللسان العريق ويلف ويدور في الأسواق والأفراح ليعود للبيوت بأوفر ربح، لسان حلو متفتح يتغنى بالموال فيهز كل جسد المنطقة بالرقص، سلس طروف لين مسرور يتقلب في أعماق الحكمة والأساطير والحكايات، فلكم غزا أبو زيد على لسان قريتي الأصقاع والمدائن فانتصر، ولكن قفز علي الزيبق فوق الأسوار وأسفل الحوائط واختفى واحتمى بلسان قريتي، وكم تجول (حسن) المغني الشهير باحثاً عن (نعيمته) وبسط له لسان قريتي السهول والوديان لينعم ويغني ويلتقي بمعشوقته،

وحتى تلك الحكاية القديمة المخيفة؛ حكاية الرجل الذي قتل أخاه ومزق جثته ووزعها على بقاع المنطقة، انتهت على لسان قريتي إلى حكاية دافئة حالمة تجمع خلالها زوجة المقتول أشلاءه المتناثرة وتعيد إليها الحياة، لا حول ولا قوة إلا باَ، فها هو لساننا العريق يتقوقع ويتقلص ويتخدر نائماً على لفافات الكلام المتهتك المتساقط في قاع الحلق، وها هي المواويل الخضراء تتيبس والتعليقات المرحة تتخثر والضحكة ذات العمق والاتساع تتهدل، ولا يبقى في الجو سوى الكأبة والفحيح.

—٣—

ولقد مر على شأن قريتي هذا زمن، قيل شهر وقيل عام وقيل قرن، قبل أن تتماسك وتصلد وتسحب حسدها المكدود بين المقابر وبيوت القديسين والاستحمام في المياه المضفدعة، لتعود إلى حقولها وبهائمها وزرعها ونخلها وكل شئونها، أضناها الجوع والعرى وسخريات القرى المجاورة، وارتج عليها الأمر أسرعت فأمسكت بزمام الأمر حتى وهو مرتج، وبدأت تدير حزينة واجفة ما تبقى من مسائلها، تحركت الأذرع والسيقان والعضلات لتدير السواقي المخربة ولتفتح القنوات وترفع التراب وتثقب الآبار وتحفر المسارب، تحركت قريتي هزيلة صامتة خرساء إلى أرضها وأشجارها وأوانيها وكوانينها وأفرانها ومرابط حيواناتها، الخرس مصيبة لكن الجوع كافر، وإذا كان الكلام ضرورة فإن حق الأمعاء أعلى من أي ضرورة، حينئذ بدأت قريتي تعيد في بطء وأسى ترتيب أوراقها؛ فإذا كان لسانها قد مات فإنٍ باقي أجهزتها قائمة حية تعمل؛ العينان والذراعان والقدمان وآلة التناسل والقلب والمخ، وعلى طاقة اللسان وقدراته أن تتسرب إلى باقي كيان الجسد، فتلجأ قريتي إلى لغتنا الأولى البدائية القديمة فتمسح عنها الغبار وتعيد إليها طلاوتها وجدتها،

الإشارة، فن الإشارة، ذلك الفن العريق الطريف، ذلك الحل الاحتياطي لأي أزمة تواجه اللسان.

وبدأت البلد تنمي فاعلية لغة الإشارة، حقاً قد تموء وتنقنق وتمط الأصوات لكنها مع حركة اليدين والحاجبين والفم وإيماءات الرأس استطاعت أن تنسى، تنسى أو تتناسى، هي على أي حال تتحرك، تتحرك بعيدًا عن ذكريات الأيام الأولى للمحنة وقبل أن تذبل آخر قدراتها على الكلام، عندما اتضح لها أن القادر على تكوين جملة يتساوى مع القادر على فركشة جملة، هي على أي حال تتحرك، تتحرك إلى بهائمها لتخرج بها إلى الهواء الطلق، وإلى مزروعاتها وأشجارها تنميها وترعاها، وإلى بيوتها تعيد بناء حوائطها المتهدمة، وإلى مصاطبها تزيلها تماماً من أمام الأبواب فلم يعد ما يدعو إلى السمر جلوساً فوقها، ثم لم تلبث أن ظهرت في الأفق مساجد بلا مآذن حيث استبدل الناس بالعقيرة المؤذنة مجرد خبطات فوق الصفيح أو الطبول داعين لأداء الفروض، ثم عظم شأن العينين والأذنين، وأصبح الإنصات لأقل أقل فحيح واجباً، والانتباه لأقل أقل حركة ضرورة، وعكفوا على فن الإشارة يطورونه ويبدعون في حركته، ليس فقط في مجرد التفاهم السريع العاجل بل وفي رواية الحكايات، حتى وصلت قريتي إلى أن تقص به الأعاجيب، حكايات أبي رجل مسلوخة والغولة والشاطر حسن والخشتبان وبدر البدور، بل ووصل الأمر أن يختزل الذراعان كل قدرات اللسان فيحكيا حتى النكتة واللغز والأحجية والنادرة، إلى أن جاء وقت على قريتي كانت تحكي نعم تحكي فيه نوادر عن رجل كان يتكلم، تماماً كما نحكي الآن نادرة عن رجل كان أخرس.

-٤-

انتعشت الحقول والشواطئ رغم ذبول اللسان، لكن تجارة قريتي بارت، نعم؛ من الممكن مثلاً أن تتعامل مرة مع تاجر أخرس، لكنك لن تستطيع التعامل كل مرة مع كل تجار القرية البكم، صحيح أن التجار حاولوا أن يستعيضوا بالأيدي عما لم يستطيعوا تبيانه بلسانهم، لكن للتجارة شأناً آخر يحتاج إلى همس وصراخ وإقناع ومسايرة، وإذا كانت قريتي لم تأخذ زمناً جسيماً لتعود إلى حقولها إلا أنها عجزت تماماً عن العودة إلى عالم التجارة، إذ أن الحقول في النهاية تحت سيطرة أهلها، أما التجارة فإنهم مجرد طرف فيها، طرف وجد مشقة وأي مشقة لإقناع الأطراف الأخرى بالعمل معه، ولا سيما وأن الأطراف الأخرى هي تلك القرى المتنافسة المتزاحمة في الوادي الواسع والتي اصطدمت كلها بقريتي أيام ذبح الطفل الأحمر الشعر، وأقوال كثيرة وردت إلينا في هذا الخصوص، منها مثلاً ما أشيع من أن التجار انهاروا ثم لم يلبثوا أن ذابوا وسط الفلاحين واندمجوا فيهم وعادوا ملاكاً أو مستأجرين أو عمال أرض، ومنها ما قيل من أن التجار تحولوا إلى مجرد وسطاء محدودي الجهد داخل معاملات أهل البلد فقط؛ ومنها مثلاً أن التجار قد هجروا قريتهم وتسللوا إلى قرى أخرى بعيدة ومتناثرة يمكن لكل قرية أن تتحمل تاجراً أخرس؛ تاجراً واحداً أخرس، وكل ذلك يعني أن قريتنا بدأت تبحر نحو الشاطئ، وأنها بدأت تبحث لها عن شئون أخرى تتفق مع كل درب تلجه، ومما يحكى أن قريتي بعد أن فقدت أسمارها ومجاليس أنسها ووجدت صعوبة في إبلاغ حكاياتها وفضائحها وشكاياها والحوادث الفردية اضطرت أن تخلق تجمعات أخرى لا لسان لها، تجمعات لها وسائلها الخاصة في الاستمتاع، ذبل اللسان وانكتم الصوت، هذا صحيح، لكن البلد لجأت إلى الأكف، إلى كفيها، تعثرت في البداية وظل الكف يخبط في الكف مؤدياً مهام صغيرة: النداء أو الاستحسان أو الرفض أو الغضب، ثم لم تلبث الأكف أن صنعت لها تصفيقاً خاصاً مريحاً

ومسلياً، فن وليد؛ فن التصفيق بدأ يدخل في دمها ونخاعها ويحل محل المواويل والحكايات والأسمار والنوادر وكل ما قد يستعان فيه بالحديث، بالحروف، بالكلام، بالرأي، بالحجة، ووجدت بلدتي ذاتها تتحقق في التصفيق، وفي تنوع التصفيق، فيكفيها التصفيق مؤونة التسلية، فتقيم به الليالي والحفلات، قد تستعين بمغن من خارجها لكن المرح والانتشاء والاندماج ينبع لا شك من تلك الأكف المدربة الفنانة الجزلة، بل وأصبح من السهل أن يقام السامر دون مغن على الإطلاق، حيث تنسال الراقصة وسط الحلقة مهتزة على وقع التصفيق السار المغموس في عمق الأعطاف والقلوب، تصفيق على الكفين وبالكفين وعلى الظهور وعلى الركب وعلى الخدود وعلى السيقان، تنويعات وإيقاعات متولدة من رغبة حقيقية أن تستمتع قريتي ولتنسى ما مر وما مضى، وحتى جاء وقت على أهل بلدتي وغزوا فيه ليالي وأفراح القرى الأخرى رغم كل الحواجز، فتجد في القرى الأخرى المغني المبدع أو الراقصة المبدعة أو العازف المبدع لكنك ستجد حتماً كل (المصفقين)من قريتي.

وما فشلت التجارة في تقديمه لقريتي نجح فيه فن التصفيق، العرس يقام في نجع وراء الجبل فيأتي المتعهد علينا ليحمل أفرادنا كي يقوموا، وأزال الفن كعادته كل التحفظ والخوف الذي حد من حركة قريتي زمناً واعترفت القرى جميعها بحق قريتي في المشاركة في أي أفراح أو مناسبات، وتعدى أمرها مجرد جوقات التصفيق إلى تدريب الغوازي وتجهيز الراقصات من بناتها الصبوحات اللدنات الجميلات، واهتز الوادي كله أمام ذلك الجمال الساحر الأخاذ الأخرس الذي يتراقص محملا بكل الإثارة، وارتاح التجار القدماء أو أحفادهم أو أحفاد أحفادهم إلى هذه السوق الجديدة التي يمكنهم أن يتسلموا في ازدهارها رزقهم فأكثرت البدل من الجوقات؛ غوازي وراقصات وزمارين ومصفقين ومنظمين ومتعهدين، وانهال المال ليعوضها عما فقدته بضياع لسانها ولم يحزنها أن يتحول خشمها إلى مجرد فتحة خربة تطلب الغذاء أو تنفس به فقط، وما كان عبثاً وعيباً أصبح في عهدها الجديد فائدة وميزة، وامتلأت قصور تجار قرى

الوادي بالمربين والمربيات من قريتي، هم وهن كاتموا أسرار البيوت وحفاظ مكنونها، هم وهن المشاهدون فقط، المغلقة أفواههم عن كل ما قد يجرح أو ما يهين أو يعيب.

— ٥ —

ووصلت المسائل الجديدة بقريتي إلى ذروة الانتعاش ثم مضى الدهر الذي كانت تنتدب فيه أبناءها وبناتها لإحياء الأفراح والأسمار حيث بدأت تتعهد هي أن تقيم الأفراح والأسمار وما قد يجد داخل مربعها، وانتشت بالميادين المزدهرة بالفرح والرقص والتصفيق والحبور، ثم لم تلبث الأفراح والسعادات أن مارت وخرجت من البيوت والميادين والشوارع إلى الخلاء، إلى الحقول، واشتهرت عائلات بتقديم أفخر الطعام، واشتهرت بيوت بتقدم أفخر الراقصات، واشتهرت أسر بتنظيم أثمن وأفخر الجلسات، وانتبهت البلد إلى العنب فجففته وقطرته، وعصرت القصب وخمرته، وحفرت جحوراً طويلة أسفل البيوت وخزنت في قبابها الجعة والعرق الزحلائي، واستطاع أفراد لهم نبوغ خاص أن يتحدثوا الكثير من وصفات تقوية الباه، وانتشر الحشيش والخشخاش وغطى مساحات واسعة من زمام أرضنا، وضاقت البيوت بأي جلسات أو مسامر فخصصت للنوم أو التصنيع على أن تكون المتعة في الهواء الطلق، هناك خارج القرية الصامتة الخضراء حيث أقيمت الخيام والعشش والشاليهات الجميلة، وحاول القمح أن ينمو فانكسرت سوقه واصطحب الأرز والذرة وانسلوا إلى بطون القنوات حيث حاولوا النمو في البقع المنزوية، ثم لم تلبث قريتنا أن رفضت هذا التسلل فحرمت في قانون مشهور زراعة المحاصيل المجهدة للأرض، وعدد القانون هذه المحرمات فشملت القمح والذرة والأرز والفاصوليا، ولم ينس القانون أن

يشجع المزروعات ذات التأثير البعيد المدى في الاقتصاد القائم(يراجع في هذا الشأن قصة عباد الشمس).

ويقول بعض المهتمين بحركة البلد في تلك الفترة إن هذا التحول قد أنتج الكثير من الضحايا، وأنا أؤكد هنا أن عدد ضحايا قريتي في تلك الفترة الهامة لم يزد عن عدد أصابع اليدين والقدمين وبعض أصابع أيدي وأقدام الجيران، والخبثاء يقصدون بالضحايا؛ هذا النوع الكسول من الفلاحين ورعاع الأرض الذين تجمدت قدراتهم عند زراعة ما لم تعد القرية في حاجة إلى زراعته، وصحيح أن البعض قد تحول إلى زراعات ظهرت أهميتها وضرورتها، لكن الكثيرين الذين أصبحوا ضحايا تمسكوا بزراعة الحبوب، وتحايل بعضهم على قانون تحريم زراعة الحبوب وتشجيع زراعة (المزاجات)، فزرعوا القمح خفية وسط نبات عباد الشمس، فاضطرت السلطات أن تجرد المنطقة نقرة نقرة ونظفت زمام القرية من كل ما رأته ضاراً من مزروعات، وقدم البعض إلى المحاكمة (فصدر الحكم بالحبس على فلاح ضبطت في حقله مجموعة من أعواد العدس، كما نفيت أسرة في القضية رقم ١٠٣٣ ج وأخرجت من القرية كلها لقيام أفرادها بتنظيم عصابة لتهريب بذور الفاصوليا، وهناك عدة قضايا متنوعة لا داعي لحصرها في هذا الحيز).

باستثناء تلك المسائل القليلة الأهمية لم يشغل قريتي شيء، تقهقر المناوئون للتقدم وانهزم عشاق الحياة الأسرية الكادحة، وانكسرت رقبة مجموعة من الأفراد، بعدها عرفت البلد طريق السعادة الحقيقي دون أدنى معارضة، وعملت على زركشة أمورها وتنسيق شئونها، والتودد التام للقرى المجاورة حيث داومت على إرسال البعثات دعاية وإعلانات عما يمكن أن تستزيد قريتي في تقديمه من وسائل متعة وترفيه لمن يقضي إجازة وسط شاليهاتها الفاخرة، يقول ه. ج. ويلز في سفره ((معالم تاريخ الإنسانية ص ٦٦٠ الكتاب السادس)) (كانت دور الحريم والترفيه مكتظة بالغواني والراقصات والمضحكين والممثلين والوسطاء والحراس، والكل يلتفون بالرواد والأغنياء يحاولون أن يحظوا

بعطف الضيوف، ذلك العطف الذي ملأ الدور رياشاً والخزائن ذهباً والعقول متعة، ولقد توقف الزمن خارج هذه البلدة رافضاً أن يقتحمها حيث لا بد أن نعيد النظر في معنى الخلود).

-٦-

في أحيان كثيرة لا نستطيع بسهولة أن نغادر أماكن نحبها ويلزمنا أن نسيح فيها، ولا سيما في قرية كقريتي مرفهة موشاة عبقة تتضوع بالخير والألوان والصمت، شريحة من الجنة، مطمح عين المستمتع ومرفأ قلبه، ولولا أني لا أثق في كثير من الروايات التي تسللت إلينا عبر الأحقاب الزمنية الطويلة لصحبتك داخل قريتي بيتاً بيتاً وشاليهاً شاليهاً، فقد حكى أن أميرها أو حاكمها أو عمدتها أو شريفها كان يحتسي على الريق كوباً معصوراً فيه أربعة خمسة من الخراف البلدية، وكان يحتفظ في بيت الظهيرة بثماني عشرة أنثى وفي بيت المساء بست وثلاثين، وقبل أن يلغي جيش القرية كان الأمير يحضر مناورات الخفراء من خيمة مزخرفة بالبنات ويقال إنه لم يكن يجد فرصة لأن يضع قدميه على الأرض، وكان يتبلغ قبل النوم بمسحوق الحشيش والسكر، وكان عادلاً نزيهاً يحب الحق والخير والجمال ويعطف على الفقراء، ومما يروى أيضاً أن مولعاً بالغريرات استقطعه الأمير أرضاً فسورها وأعشبها وأشجرها ثم جهزها بجحور وأكمات، وأطلق فيها الكثير من البنات حيث كانت المتعة تصل إلى ذروتها في هذا الجو الوحشي الشبق، وحاول كاتب أو اثنان أن يرصدا ذلك الواقع المنتشي لكن الرقيب على أوراق البردي أشار بأن يبدأ كتاباتهم بملاحظة أن هذه الوقائع حدثت في العهود الماضية قبل أن يشل لسان القرية، فلما رفض الكتاب ذلك أمر بطردهم ليموتوا في المنفى.

وكانت حفلات القرية الضاجة الصاخبة المزمرة الخرساء تنتهي قبل الفجر ليتسنى إنهاء رغباتهم المتفق عليها قبل ظهر اليوم التالي، وبلغ حد الشبع

الصامت في قريتي أن فقدت الكلاب كلوبتها وتحولت إلى مجرد حيوانات هاشة متثائبة تخطو فوقها الثعالب وأحيانًا تداعبها، وكان يحلو للرواد والضيوف أن يختطفوا البنات من الشوارع، مرحين أو جادين أو محاولين كسر حدة الملل، إن ذلك يحقق لهم على أية حال نوعاً من المتعة، وعند اقتيادهم لمخفر الأمير كان رجال الأمير يقدمون الاعتذارات والهدايا للمتهمين وينذرون الخرساوات الجميلات بعدم إحداث شغب مستقبلاً، ومن الحوادث النبيلة التي أسر بها لنا التاريخ أن رجلاً قتل زوجته لإنجابها خمسة ذكور دون إناث، وقيل إن رجل وأد الأولاد في حقل خشخاش، وعند محاكمته على سلوكه تعلل بخوفه من خراب البيت مستقبلاً، وقد قبل الحاكم تعليله ومنح تعويضاً.

—٧—

وفجأة يتوقف المؤرخون والرواة وناقلوا الأخبار، يتوقفون والبلد في قمة عزها، كل تطويرها وازدهارها وما قدمته لحركة الإنسان ينقطع ولا نلمح له أثراً في أوراق أو ألسنة أو عقول، هل ضاعت القرية المضيئة الجزلة في مسارات الزمن الشرس؟ وكيف ضاعت؟، وقبل أن نتعرض لشتى النهايات المفترضة التي حاقت بقريتي، نتوقف قليلاً عند حادث وجد مهملاً وسط آلاف من الشوائب والأكاذيب؛ فقد روى أن رجلاً عتي السحنة تسلل إلى القرية وظل زمناً يجوس في شوارعها وأزقتها وطرقاتها وجنباتها وشاليهاتها، ولم يدهش القرية في الرجل الغريب إلا انصرافه المطلق عن مباهجها ومراقصها وملذاتها، ولم يستمر اندهاشها طويلاً، فقد رأته يقيس عتبات بيوت، ويحفر تحت بعض الجدران، وظلت القرية ناظرة للغريب بنصف عين حتى تشكى بعض الرواد من اعتراضه طريق لهوهم، واضطرت القرية أن تنذره تمهيداً لإبعاده لكن الرجل اختفى، ثم نمى إلى علم حاكمها أن الرجل قادم من جبال أطلس، وأنه موفد من جنها لفك

(الرصد) وحل (العمل) تمهيداً لإطلاق سراح لسان البلد، واستطاع البصاصون تحديد مكان الغريب القادم من جبال أطلس، وانتشر خبر في القرية أن الغريب قد استحوذ على بعض أطفالها وأنه يربيهم وسط دغل بين المقابر، وكمنت البلد للرجل وفاجأته بحصار وجذبته من وكره، وضبطت لديه طفلين واعترف الرجل بكلام أخرق مؤداه أنه أخذ على عاتقه تعليم الطفلين الكلام؛ الكلام ؟.

وترددت أخبار أن الحصار وصل إلى مداه، وأن الساحر القادم من جبال الجن قد انتهك وتمزق أسفل الأحذية الذهبية، وتمزق الطفلان أيضاً وأن الجن بعد ذلك قامت بمهاجمة البلدة فدكتها وجعلت من عاليها واطيها، وقيل إن ذلك لم يحدث وأن ريحاً صرصراً عاتية قد هاجمت البلد في الخماسين فمزقتها ومحتها، وقيل إن قوماً حمقى حانقين هاجموا البلدة وأبادوها، وقيل إن نوعاً من النمل قد تكاثر في أقبية البيوت ثم فاض في الشوارع والطرقات والأجساد والمأكولات فافترسها، وقيل... وقيل... لكن المؤكد أن القرية اختفت أو اندثرت، وأن حيز الأرض الذي كانت تشغله ما زال حتى اليوم مجرد بقعة رطبة سوداء مقفرة تئز فيها الزنابير وتعشعش فيها الحشرات وتخلو تماماً من كل نبات وعندما تسير فوق أديمها يمكن لك إذا أنصت أن تسمع أصواتًا تحت الأرض تموء وتنقنق، وأثناء احتسائنا لبعض المشروبات الذهبية في شاليه خلف الهرم نبهنا مؤرخ معاصر بأن القرية ما زالت فوق الأرض أيضاً لكنه عجز عن تحديد موقعها، فقد كان في حالة سكر بين.

الفرسان يعشقون الطيور

محمد مستجاب

ارتعش النهار فأسقط أعشاش العصافير في أتون النار، وثب الحزن يساراً وأهال التراب فوق جثث الأطفال، ضجت المدن من الضحك والترانيم والبلاهة والمسرة، انهارت أفران القرى فوق الطواجن والخبز المقمر، قالت امرأة تحب الكلاب وتقتني الثعالب "إياكم وهذا الوجه الأسود الفج فإنه يورث العقم وينشر السفاح ويجادل في الحق ويدمر شرانق الحرير ويتاجر فيجلود العذارى ويجلب الكمد ويتشهى بالنكد".

ارتعش النهار فأسقط أعشاش العصافير في أتون النار، ظلت الغربان تضحك حتى ابيضت قوادمها ومناقيرها وأطراف أجنحتها، تشققت بطون الترع فتعملقت الحلفاء والداتورة والسحالي، تراقص النمل حول ضروع الأبقار، استل الفارس حسامه وامتطى أدهمه، تحلق أطفال الفقراء حوله فمنحهم الابتسامات والإصرار والسلوان والحلوى، اخترق الفارس الجموع والشوارع والأحزان حتى أدرك قصر فاتنة الزمان، كان الجو ربيعاً والحزن دافئاً والكمد متوقداً، أيتها الفاتنة الشريرة الحمقاء المتربعة على عرش القرية إني قادم إليك لأقتص من امتصاصك الدموي لأرزاق الفقراء، هاجمت

الجماهير غضباً فتشبثت الأشجار ببقايا الخضرة وتصارعت مياه النهر مع شقوق الجفاف، تلاصق الحراس بأسوار القصر مستعدين للدفاع عن الفاتنة، أطلت الفاتنة الجميلة من مقصورتها فانفجر الناس غيظاً وأحجاراً وصراخاً وطوباً، لكن الفاتنة وقفت راسخة، ازدادت الجموع تماسكاً وتضامناً حول الفارس، ظلت ابتسامة الفاتنة تتسع حتى شملت الخراف والسواقي والأطفال والأفران والجماهير والأناشيد والمواويل، تقدم الفارس خطوته الأخيرة مصمماً على إنهاء حساب السنوات المريرة، تحركت الجماهير خلف الفارس حاملين أطفالهم فوق أكتافهم، أشاحت الفاتنة بذراعها، توقفت الحشود، ازداد الحراس تكاتفاً استعداداً للفتك بالجماهير، صرخت الفاتنة بصوتها الغاضب الحنون، أعرف مطالبكم لكني أحذركم من الدم ما ذنب الحراس والجماهير أن يتقاتلوا إني مستعدة للتباحث في الأمر، تقدم الفارس، وفي الظهيرة بدأ التباحث وفي المساء أعلن الزواج، فانتشت الجماهير مرحاً واغتباطاً وفرحاً وابتهاجاً وفي اليوم الرابع خرجت الفاتنة من قصرها ساحبة خلفها جسد الفارس العتيد المضمخ بالعطور، ظلت تجره في الشوارع حتى سويقة القرية، ووسط الميدان فرشت جسد الفارس المضمخ بالعطور وقطعت رأسه.

وثب الحزن يساراً وأهال التراب فوق جثث الأطفال، ضجت المدن من الضحك والترانيم والبلاهة والمسرة، زحف السنط مغتالاً ثمار التوت، انطفأت الكوانين وتسلقت الكلاب الأسرة والفراش والمقاعد، استرخت الثعابين في جحور الأرانب، طنت الزنابير حول الأزيار، التف الفقراء حول الرواة والقصاصين ومرتلي الأوردة وصانعي التمائم، عجت البطون بالديدان، استل ابن الفارس حسامه وامتطى أدهمه، تحلق أطفال الفقراء حوله فمنحهم الابتسامات والإصرار والسلوان والحلوى، اخترق الفارس الجموع والشوارع والأحزان حتى أدرك قصر فتنة الزمان، كان الجو ر بيعاً والحزن دافئاً والكمد متوقداً، أيتها الفاتنة الشريرة الحمقاء المتربعة على عرش القرية إني قادم إليك لأقتص، وأشاحت الفاتنة بذراعها، وفي الظهيرة بدأ التباحث وفي المساء أعلن

الزواج فانتشت الجماهير مرحاً واغتباطاً وفرحاً وابتهاجاً، وفي اليوم الرابع خرجت الفاتنة من قصرها ساحبة خلفها جسد الفارس العتيد المضمخ بالعطور، ظلت تجره في الشوارع حتى سويقة القرية، ووسط الميدان فرشت جسد الفارس المضمخ بالعطور وقطعت رأسه.

انهارت الأفران فوق الطواحن والخبز المقمر، انغلقت الأفواه وانفتحت وبدأ لعابها يسيل، التوى التعقل يميناً ويساراً، ثم انكفأ داخل جمجمة، باضت الخراف وجفت الأمعاء ونما الورد كرنباً، انحشر الحب ركاماً في أنابيب المبايض، داعب الهالوك الفول الهزيل بأبيات من أشعار الحكمة، أوعز ملاك للرب أن يوقف المهزلة، ترهلت السحب وكلحت وتشكت من انعدام المياه، تلوت السراديب خراباً وامتدت في أعماق الشرايين، ظلت المرأة التي تحب الكلاب وتقتني الثعالب المواعظ بالملائكة، استل حفيد الفارس حسامه وامتطى أدهمه، وفي الظهيرة بدأ التباحث.

الجبارنة

محمد مستجاب

اختلج صوت الجبارنة حزناً، أشار إليهم جابر الكبير المسجى رامشاً أن يجلسوا همس واحداً باكياً أوصنا يا أبانا، فظل جابر الكبير ممعناً وصامتاً، أسرع واحد فجمع أعواداً في حزمة واحدة ليذكرهم بأن الاتحاد قوة فظل جابر الكبير ممعناً وصامتاً، تهدج صوت آل جابر بترنيمة عن وزير بدأ حياته في جب فظل جابر الكبير ممعناً وصامتاً، تقلب وجه الجبارنة في الأركان والسقف والفراش ثم في وجه جابر الكبير المشع نوراً، أوصنا يا أبانا، وقبل أن ينغلق رمش عين جابر الكبير همس في قوة "أوصيكم باقتناء جمل".

ووفود المعزين تتمتم صبراً وسلواناً، الرب أخذ والرب يعطي، طوال عمر الجبارنة ما فكروا في جمل، وتصدر جابر الكبير مأتم جابر الكبير فظل الجمل يهوم متشكلاً ضاغطاً تسرب من الوصية إلى الهمس، وكل هنيهة يقترب فم جابر نحو أذن جابر، الرب أخذ والرب يعطي، فمنذ أن أصبح لذوات الأربع أربع ونجع الجبارنة يحب الحمير، يمتطي الحمير ويقص شعر الحمير ويصبغ الحمير ويلجم الحمير، يقلم الأظلاف ويصنع البراذع وزنابيل السباخ، ويداوي الظهور ويكافح التسلح وكسور الركب وتآكل الحوافر، وأي جابر يحبو يمكنه

ومن النظرة الأولى أن يعرف نوع أي حمار، وسنه وعدد الحدوات التي أهلكها وموطنه الأصلي، وما حاق به من تجارب منذ نعومة حوافره، الرب أخذ والرب يعطي، وما كاد المأتم ينفض حتى أيقن نصف الجبارنة أن جبران العمودي عاش خمسة وثلاثين عاماً ناسكاً متوحداً فوق عمود بسبب خلو النجع من الجمال، جمل شامخ ساقم، وكانت الجمال تعبر الصحراء حاملة للرهبان المنقطعين الخبز والحطب والصبر والقدرة، واستظل الأنبان « جراباموں » بجملة اتقاء الهجير ثم نحره جوعاً فبكى الجمل راضياً، ثم أيقن النصف الباقي من الجبارنة أنهم ليسوا كأولاد عبدالمعز الذين وهبوا حياتهم للماعز، أو آل مفتاح الذي يسيحون في النجوع ليصلحوا مغاليق الأبواب، كما أنهم بعد اليوم لن يكونوا كتلك الجماعات المعروفة التي وقعت في براثن الدجاج أو الأرانب أو فتح المندل أو دق طبول الزار أو صنع التمائم أو سرقة أكفان الموتى أو تجليخ المقصات والسكاكين، جمل، شكراً للرب أولاً ثم لجابر الراحل بعده.

وظهر أول جمل قادماً من سواكن أو سمالوط أو درب الأربعين أو سيوة، أطل على النجع بسنامه العالي ورقبته الشامخة ورأسه المتطلع إلى السحب، وتدفق صوته المشابه لصوت اندفاع المياه من القلة، هادئاً صبوراً يسير الهوينى على بساط الرحمة وسرت موجة الحبور في الجبارنة فاهتزوا وتقافزوا وتعلق جبير في الرقبة العالية، وتسلق جبران سنام الجمل لكنه سقط، وتعابثت جبرانة في الذيل القصير فازداد النجع مرحاً ومار آل جابر بالنشاط والسعادة، وكل يوم يمر تفد الجمال إلى النجع ومع كل جمل يفد يكتشف الجبارنة اللحم والشموخ والوبر ويكتشفون ما عانوه داخل تلك البيوت الكابية والحارات الكابية، فقام الجبارنة بهدم أصداغ البيوت وتوسيعها وقاموا بفرش الرمل في الأفنية والباحات، وقامت جبيرة باختلاق مغزل يثير الضحك لكنه أنتج من الوبر خيوطاً وتجمعت الخيوط في آخر الأمر تلفيحة على عنق جبرانها، فقام جبور أريب بتركيب نول فامتلأ النجع بالزعابيط والتلافيح والأغطية والدفء، وقام جبارة قديم بتعليم الصغار كيف ظهر الهوادج.

وانتشى النجع حينما زف أول عروس في حياته على ظهر جمل، كانوا في ذلك العصر الذي لا يميلون إلى التفكير فيه ينقلون العرائس من بيت لبيت دون تلك الفرحة القصوى التي تشع، الهودج المنمق المزخرف والعروس فوقه تتلألأ وتتألق والجمل تحتها يتهادى، وتنطلق الأعيرة النارية فلا يفزع، وتنطلق الزغاريد فلا يفزع، وتشتعل النيران فلا يفزع، وتنذبح الجمال كرماً وحفاوة فلا يفزع، حتى أن من تزوج من قبل صمم على أن يعيد الاحتفال بزواجه من جديد وخلال سنوات قليلة امتزج الجبارنة بالجمال وامتزجت الجمال بالجبارنة، ارتفعت أسقف بيوتهم وارتدوا الحبرة والكوفية والمراكب الأنيقة، وبارزوا العربان في صناعة الهوادج وتنميقها، ونجحوا في اكتشاف مزيج جديد لعلاج الجرب، وتمكنوا من حفظ اللحوم المتبلة شهوراً، وقام جابران متجاوران بتخزين الدهون وبهريز العظام، وتمكن جبرون من احتكار جلود الجمال وأجاد تسويقها في النجوع المترامية في الوادي، ونجح جبرة صبور في استحداث علاجات للبهاق من أحشاء الجمل، وللصمم من طبلة أذن الجمل، وللسير أثناء النوم من خف الجمل، ولاضطراب الدورة الشهرية من نخاع الجمل، وللتزود بالثقة ليلة الزفاف من حليل الجمل، ثم نجح جبرة أكثر صبراً في تجفيف عروق الجمل وسحقها مع الوبر المحروق وشحم مؤخر الرقبة ليصل إلى مزيج لعلاج العقم فازداد النجع شموخاً، وفخراً، وزهواً، حتى أن أجساد الجبارنة استطالت ورقابهم علت وشابت أصواتهم غنة تدفق المياه من القلل، غلظت عيونهم وقصرت آذانهم ثم لم تلبث مشافرهم أن انشقت وأقدامهم أن تفلطحت.

اختلج صوت الجبارنة حزناً، أشار إليهم جابر الكبير المسجى رامشاً أن يجلسوا همس واحداً باكياً، أوصنا يا أبانا، فظل جابر الكبير ممعناً وصامتاً، أسرع أحدهم فجمع أعواداً في حزمة واحدة ليذكرهم بأن الاتحاد قوة فظل جابر الكبير ممعناً وصامتاً، وتهدج صوت آل جابر بترنيمة عن وزير بدأ حياته في جب فظل جابر الكبير ممعًنا وصامتاً، رتل ذو صوت صادح حكاية المبتلى في جسده بالقروح فحملته زوجته إلى الأصقاع بحثاً عن علاج فظل جابر

الكبير صامتاً، أنشد ذو صوت رخيم موعظة الجمل الذي جاب الفيافي بحثاً عن قاتل صاحبه فظل جابر الكبير ممعناً وصامتاً، تقلب وجه الجبارنة في الأركان والسقف والفراش ثم في وجه جابر الكبير المشع نوراً، أوصنا يا أبانا.

وقبل أن ينغلق رمش عين جابر الكبير همس في قوة "أوصيكم باقتناء جمل"، نجع طاهر ابن طاهر من أصلاب أطهار، كيف فات عليه أمر البغال؟، وبمجرد الانتهاء من قبول العزاء في جابر الكبير كان النجع ينظر بنصف عين إلى الجمال الباركة، حجمها الضخم وعيونها الغبية ورقابها الملتوية، وهمس جبور في أذن جبور"الرب أخذ والرب يعطي، تصور لم أستطع أن أذوق لحومها أبداً؟"، ووقف جبران على هودج مركون وحمد الرب، والجمل كما تعرفون ابن صحراء ونحن نعيش في وديان، وابن جبرانة الوحيد فتك به جمل خلصناه يا عيني أشلاء من حنك القاعود، وقبل أن تتفاعل العقول مع الذكريات الأليمة ظهر البغل وديعاً أطل هادئاً تحرك وكأنه قادم من منازل القمر وقامت جبيرة مزغردة ونثرت الدقيق على الوجه الرصين واهتز وجدان الجبارنة فأطلقوا النيران والأقوال والحكم، وكل بغل يفد يكتشفون فيه الخصال والميزات، اعتمد عليه الأنبياء في رحلاتهم المرهقة إلى عنان السماء، وشارك العلماء في اختراقهم المضني لصحراوات تونس وأسبانيا والنمسا والبنغال، حمل الكتب والقوارير والخيام أحقاباً طويلة ما سمعنا أبداً أن جملاً تمكن من اجتياز قناة، الرب أخذ والرب يعطي، وما سمعنا أبداً أن جملاً صعد جبلاً، دعونا من الجمال ولا داعي لإثارة الشجن أو توجيه اللوم نحن أثناء اليوم، فصرخ جبران مكلوم أن يتقوا الرب ويتركوا الخلق يقولون الحق، ثم علا صوته وتدفق مغرقاً المكان "أي واحد منكم ذلك الذي ينسى واقعة فرن جبرون الطيب؟"، والجبارنة أناس طيبون لكن الأمر صحيح، فقد كان جبرون الطيب عائداً في ذاك اليوم ممتطياً قاعوده الأثير، وعند انحناءة البيت الكبير هاج القاعود، هاج وتلاطم في الجدران واندفع في الشوارع عاصفة وجبرون الطيب متشبثاً بظهره يصرخ، والجبارنة ينظرون من الأبواب والكوات ويضحكون ثم تمكن القاعود الهائج من قذف جسد جبرون

ليصكه في حائط لتنكسر رقبته، واستمر القاعود يخترق حتى اقتحم بيت صاحبه فانهارت الجدران على آل جبرون الطيب، وظل القاعود يدك المكان بسيقانه وعوارضه حتى انهار الفرن واشتعلت النيران، وماذا يا جبران المكلوم؟ ومع ذلك ظل الجبارنة يضحكون، حينئذ ثار جبير صامتاً واندفع إلى جمله فعقره إثباتاً لكراهيته لمثل هذا الحيوان، وكاد النجع يتحول إلى مذبحة لولا أن البغال استمرت تهل.

وارتاح البغال في نجع الجبارنة، وتحول بسرعة إلى همة ونشاط وجر وشحن، وقام أربعة جبرانات بفتح ورشة عربات وساعدوا جبوراً مكافحاً كي يصبح حداداً وجبوراً متسلقا أن يصبح نجاراً، واستحالت الباحات والأفنية والأحواش إلى أماكن تجميع سطوح وعجلات وعرائس العربات، وانتشى الجبارنة وهم يرون بغالهم تخترق الطرق ساحبة خلفها العربات إلى كل النجوع المجاورة، ولأول مرة عرف النجع تمهيد الطرق وتسويتها، وأجاد معرفة نوع الشجر والخشب والحديد، وظهر منهم نابغون في مداواة الجراح وتركيب الحدوات وبذل خراريج البغال، وظهرت بيوت متخصصة في السروج والركابات والتحزيم والتعريش، وقام منظرون بتوجيه الجبارنة إلى أحسن طرق مغاداة جراح الاحتكاك وأورام القوائم وتسلخات الظهور، وكلما عج النجع بالبغال والعربات ازداد الجبارنة زهواً واكتنازاً واندفعت طهارة البغل إلى السلوك والكلام، أي عصر ذاك الذي جعلهم يتجمعون حول حمارة وحمار يسعيان للتواصل؟، وأي فجاجة تلك التي كانت تؤذي عيونهم بمنظر ناقة مبطوئة أرضاً وجملها يرغي ويزيد رغبة فيها، فلنردم الذكرى ولنسعد بالجبارنة وهم يمارسون حياة نقية دون تعشير وعسس وتوليد وقاذورات وألقت الطهارة ظلها على النجع كله فأصبح هادئاً مستكيناً يثابر ويتاجر ويتقاسم الرزق، وبدا آل جابر موفوري الصحة سليمي الأسنان والقواطع ولم يعد لأحد منهم صوت منفر كأنكر الأصوات أو حنجرة مجلجلة كانسكاب المياه من القلل، فلم يكن البغل ضاجاً أو مزعجاً، صوته ناعم رقيق ليس نهيقاً ولا ثغاء، إنما هو هذا الصوت

اللين الرقيق المشابه للهسيس، مجرد هسيس غير مقلق حتى كاد الجبارنة يحسون أنهم لم يناموا طوال حياتهم إلا الآن، وانكمشت حناجرهم وتضخمت أكتافهم واستطالت مناخيرهم وسمنت كواهلهم ومؤخراتهم، وبدا أن الجر والشحن والنقل والتخزين والترتيب والمتاجرة قد داست على ذلك الشوق الموروث للزوجة والأنجال، وأصبح سهلاً على أي جابر أن يتوغل في النجوع أياماً وشهوراً دون قلق أو توجس، وبدأت أقوالهم ومواويلهم وأشعارهم تخلص من رذائل العشق والعوازل والخيانة والهيام، وانتفت من حكاياتهم هذه المباذل التي أغرقتهم فيها عصور البذاءات، ثم لم يلبث الجبارنة أن توغلوا أكثر في عالم الرصانة والحكمة المبطن بالهدوء والنوم دون ضجيج الأحلام.

رتل ذو صوت صادح حكاية المبتلى في جسده بالقروح فحملته زوجته إلى الأصقاع بحثاً عن علاج فظل جابر الكبير صامتاً، أنشد ذو صوت رخيم موعظة الجمل الذي جاب الفيافي بحثاً عن قاتل صاحبه فظل جابر الكبير ممعناً وصامتا، انطلق هسيس ذو شجن يحكي عن بغل صادق ظل يسحب عربته خلفه دون أن يدرك أنها قد انفصلت وسقطت بصاحبها في مستنقع فظل جابر الكبير ممعناً وصامتاً، تقلب وجه الجبارنة في الأركان والسقف والفراش ثم في وجه جابر الكبير المشع نوراً، أوصنا يا أبانا، وقبل أن ينغلق رمش عين جابر الكبير همس في قوة "أوصيكم باقتناء حلوف".

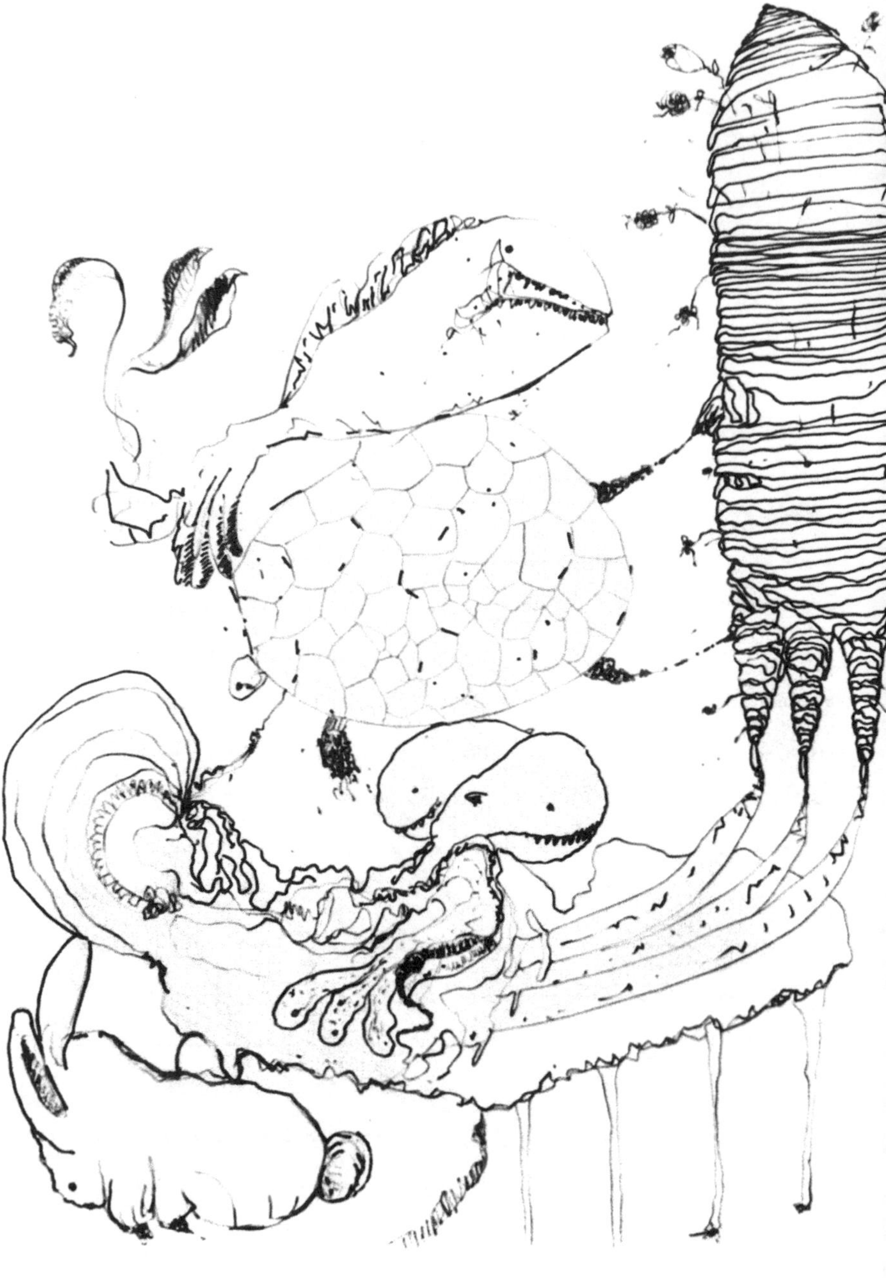

وائل شوقي (مواليد ١٩٧١)
ولد وائل شوقي في الإسكندرية، مصر، حيث لا يزال يعيش ويعمل هناك، وتشمل ممارسته الفنية أعمال الفيديو والفيلم والرسم والعروض الأدائية. تقلد العديد من المعارض الفردية دولياً في متحف هامر، الولايات المتحدة الأمريكية (٢٠١٣)، ومعهد كنست ورك، ألمانيا (٢٠١٢)، ومتحف نوتنغهام المعاصر، المملكة المتحدة (٢٠١١)، ومركز ذا والكر للفنون، الولايات المتحدة الأمريكية (٢٠١١)، وسيتا ديلارتي، إيطاليا (٢٠١٠)، وكونستهاله فينترتور، سويسرا (٢٠٠٧)، ورابطة الفن لودفيغسبورغ، ألمانيا (٢٠٠٥). كما شارك في بينالي الشارقة ١١ (٢٠١٣)، وفي دوكومنتا ١٣ (٢٠١٢)، وبينالي اسطنبول ٢٠٠٥، وبينالي البندقية في ٢٠٠٣. في ٢٠١١ تلقى جائزة "مؤسسة شيرينغ للفنون"، وفي ٢٠١٢ تلقى جائزة أبراج كابيتال. إلى جانب عمله كفنان أسس شوقي مؤسسة "ماس الإسكندرية" للتعليم الفني، كأول استوديو وبرنامج دراسي مستقل للفنانين الصاعدين في الإسكندرية، مصر. في ٢٠١١ وفي إطار برنامج الفنان المقيم شارك شوقي ضمن برنامج الشاهد في مؤسسة الشارقة للفنون وفي مشروع طريق أدجوار في سربنتاين، الذي نظم بالتعاون مع غاليري تاون هاوس، القاهرة، ومؤسسة دلفينا، لندن.

محمد مستجاب (١٩٣٨ – ٢٠٠٥)

ولد محمد مستجاب في ديروط في صعيد مصر، حصل على الشهادة الثانوية، إلا أنه عمل في مجمع اللغة العربية في القاهرة ليصبح لاحقاً المدير العام. نشر مستجاب أول قصة قصيرة له بعنوان الوصية الحادية عشر في مجلة الهلال في عام ١٩٦٩. وتلقى عن روايته الأولى "من التاريخ السري لنعمان عبد الحافظ" (١٩٨٣) جائزة الدولة التشجيعية المصرية في عام ١٩٨٤، وتم اختياره كواحدة من أفضل مئة رواية عربية في القرن العشرين. وأدرجت في مجموعة من القصص القصيرة حكايات من ديروط (١٩٨٤) التي ترجمت إلى اللغة الإنجليزية ونشرت من قبل الجامعة الأمريكية في القاهرة عام ٢٠٠٨.

نود أن نتقدم بالشكر لكل من ساهم في هذا الكتاب وفي المعارض، مثمنين جهودهم، وهم: محمد مستجاب، الذي تكرم بإعطائنا الإذن لإعادة طباعة قصص والده الثلاث التي ألهمت أفلام العرابة المدفونة، وفينر فيستوشن لدعمهم في إنتاج العرابة المدفونة الثاني، وأندريه صفير زملر وآنا نوفالك في غاليري صفير زملر، ونيكولاس لوجسديل وغريغ هيلتي في غاليري ليسون، و المدير سوزان فيفر والقيَم نينا تاباسومي في فريدرسيانم في كاسل، ونيل هيوسن، المدير المساعد لبرامج التحرير، وياسمين جادو، مدير الحقوق والعقود، وسهى محسن في الجامعة الأمريكية بالقاهرة، وريم شديد، نائب المدير في مؤسسة الشارقة للفنون، وفريق مؤسسة الشارقة للفنون، وجوشن فولز، رئيس البرامج، وريبيكا لوين، قيَم معارض، ومايك كوغان، مدير غاليري، وفريق غاليري سربنتاين، وهاني شرف، وكارين مارتا، وداستن كوسنتينو، وكوين وينجتون من كارين مارتا لاستشارات التحرير.

جوليا بيتون جونز
مدير، غاليرهات سيربنتاين، ومدير مشارك للمعارض والبرامح

هانس أولريخ أوبريست
مدير مشارك للمعارض والبرامج ومدير المشروعات الدولية

حور القاسمي
رئيس، مؤسسة الشارقة للفنون

الفرسان يعشقون العطور وحكايات أخرى

وائل شوقي

تحرير
كارين مارتا
منسق التحرير
جوشن فولز، ريم شديد، ريبيكا لوين
تصميم
هاني شرف
مراجعة اللغة الإنجليزية
ماري لينر
ترجمة
ناصر ونوس
مراجعة وتحرير اللغة العربية
نور الرفاعي
مساعد التحرير
كوين وينجتون

طبع في الشارقة، مطبعة نبيل

جميع الأعمال الفنية لوائل شوقي، ٢٠١٣

الاقتباس في الصفحة ٧ أخذ من محمد مستجاب، الجبارنة.

تم إنتاج العرابة المدفونة الثاني بالتعاون بين

Wiener Festwochen

ISBN 978-1-908617-17-0
غاليرهات سيربنتاين

ISBN 978-9948-444-81-7
مؤسسة الشارقة للفنون

ISBN 978-3-86335-487-9
كتب كوينغ

نشر:

مؤسسة الشارقة للفنون
منطقة الفنون
ص ب ١٩٩٨٩، الشارقة
الإمارات العربية المتحدة
www.sharjahart.org

غاليري سيربنتاين
حدائق كنسينغتون
لندن W٢ ٣XA
هاتف ٦٠٧٥ ٧٤٠٢ ٢٠ (٠) ٤٤+
فاكس ٤١٠٣ ٧٤٠٢ ٢٠ (٠) ٤٤+
www.serpentinegalleries.org

كتب كونيغ المحدودة
في غاليرهات سيربنتاين
حدائق كنسينغتون
لندن W٢ ٣XA
www.koenigbooks.co.uk

توزيع:

أوروبا
مكتبة فالتر كونيغ، كولن
إهرنستر، ٤، ٥٠٦٧٢، كولن
هاتف ٥٣-٦ ٥٩ ٢٠ /٢٢١ (٠) ٤٩+
فاكس ٦٠-٦ ٥٩ ٢٠ /٢٢١ (٠) ٤٩+
verlag@buchhandlung-walther-koenig.de

المملكة المتحدة وجمهورية ايرلندا
كورنرهاوس للمنشورات
٧٠ شارع أكسفورد
GB مانشستر M١ ٥NH
هاتف ١٥٠٣ ٢٠٠ ١٦١ (٠) ٤٤+
فاكس ١٥٠٤ ٢٠٠ ١٦١ (٠) ٤٤+
publications@cornerhouse.org

الإمارات العربية المتحدة
مؤسسة الشارقة للفنون
منطقة الفنون
ص ب ١٩٩٨٩، الشارقة
الإمارات العربية المتحدة
www.sharjahart.org

الأمريكتان
ARTBOOK | D.A.P.
١٥٥ الجادة السادسة، الطابق الثاني
نيويورك، NY ١٠٠١٣
هاتف ١٩٩٩-٦٢٧-٢١٢ ١+
فاكس ٩٤٨٤-٦٢٧-٢١٢ ١+
orders@dapinc.com
www.artbook.com

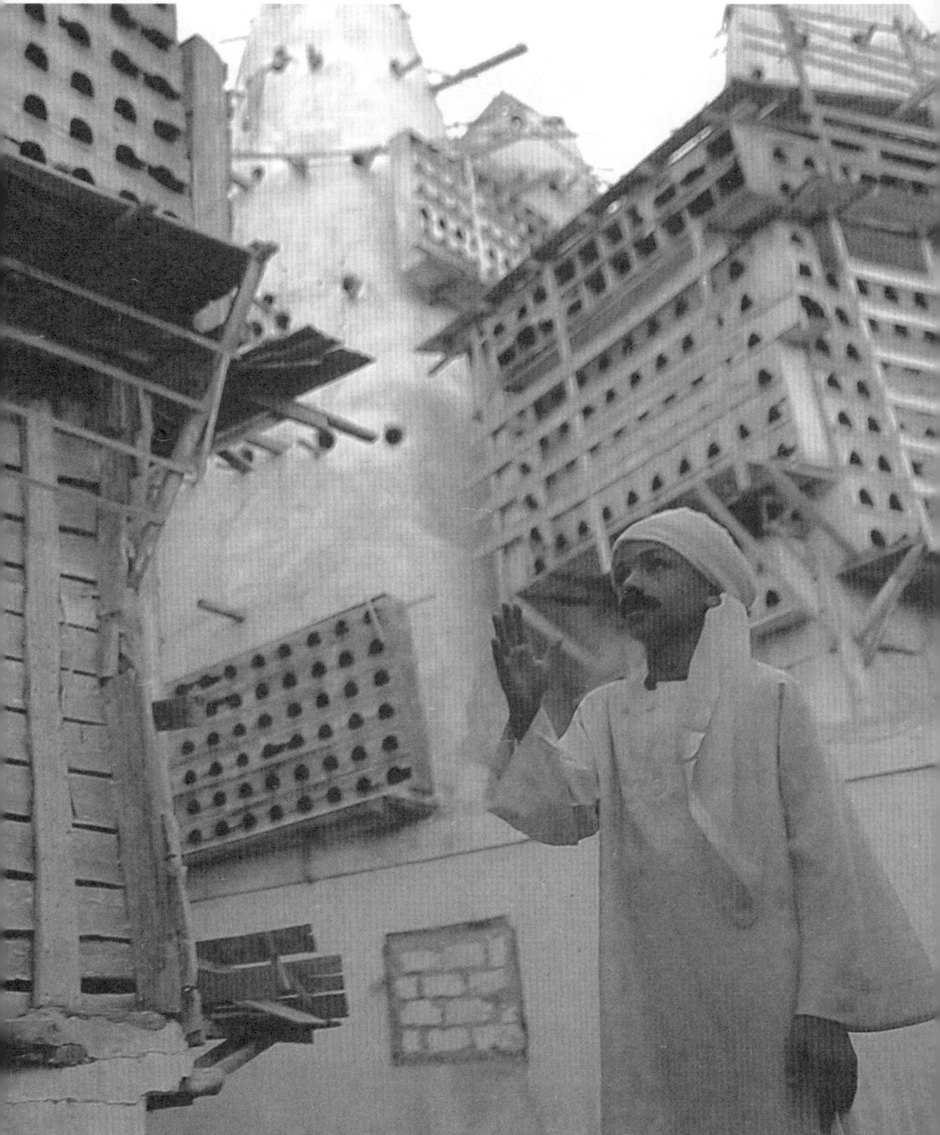

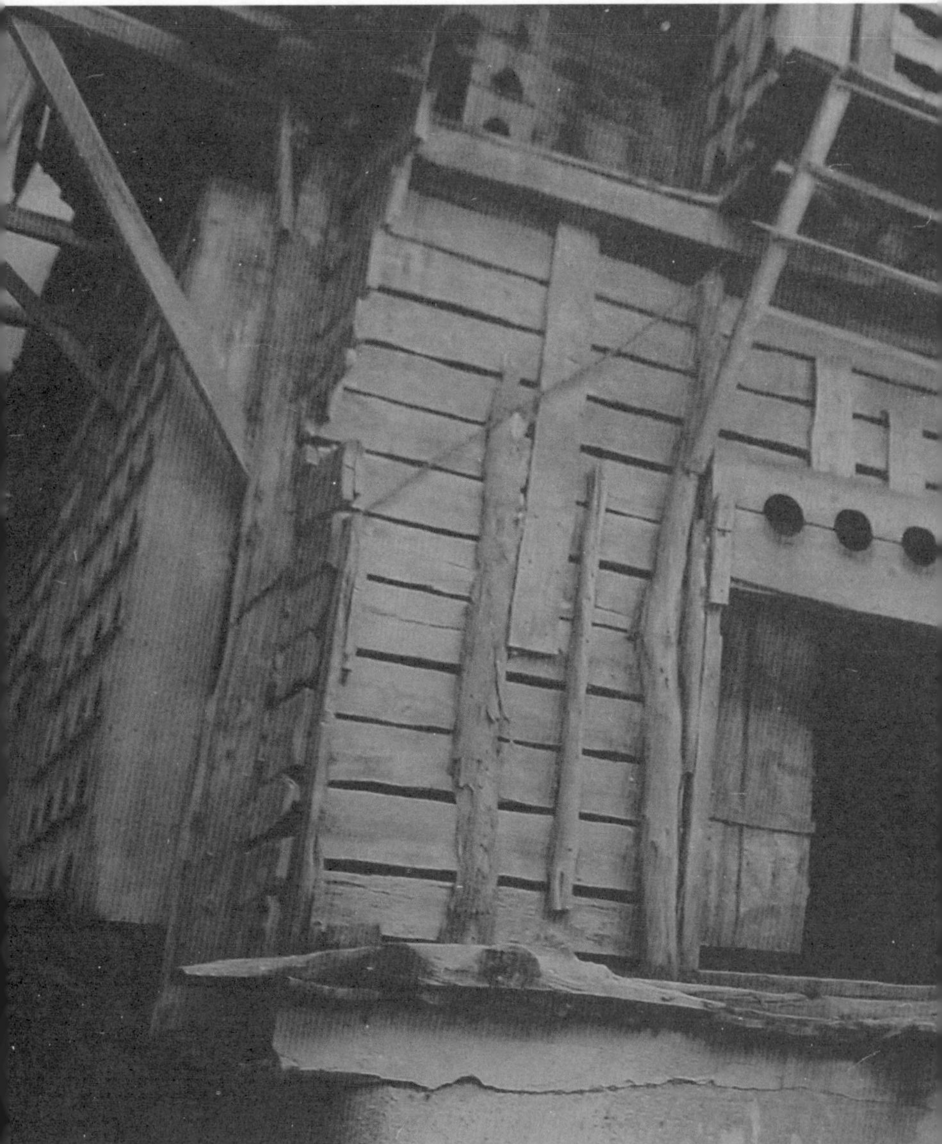

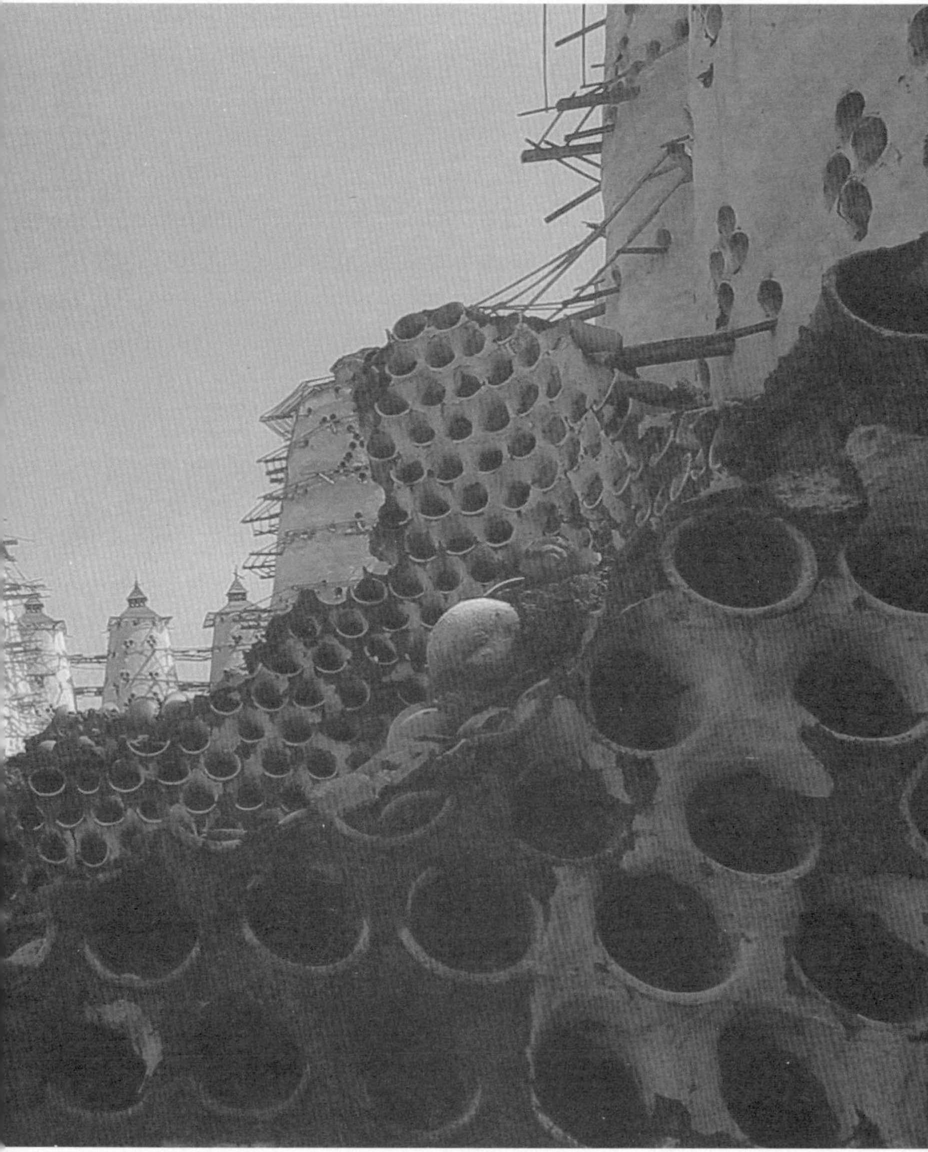

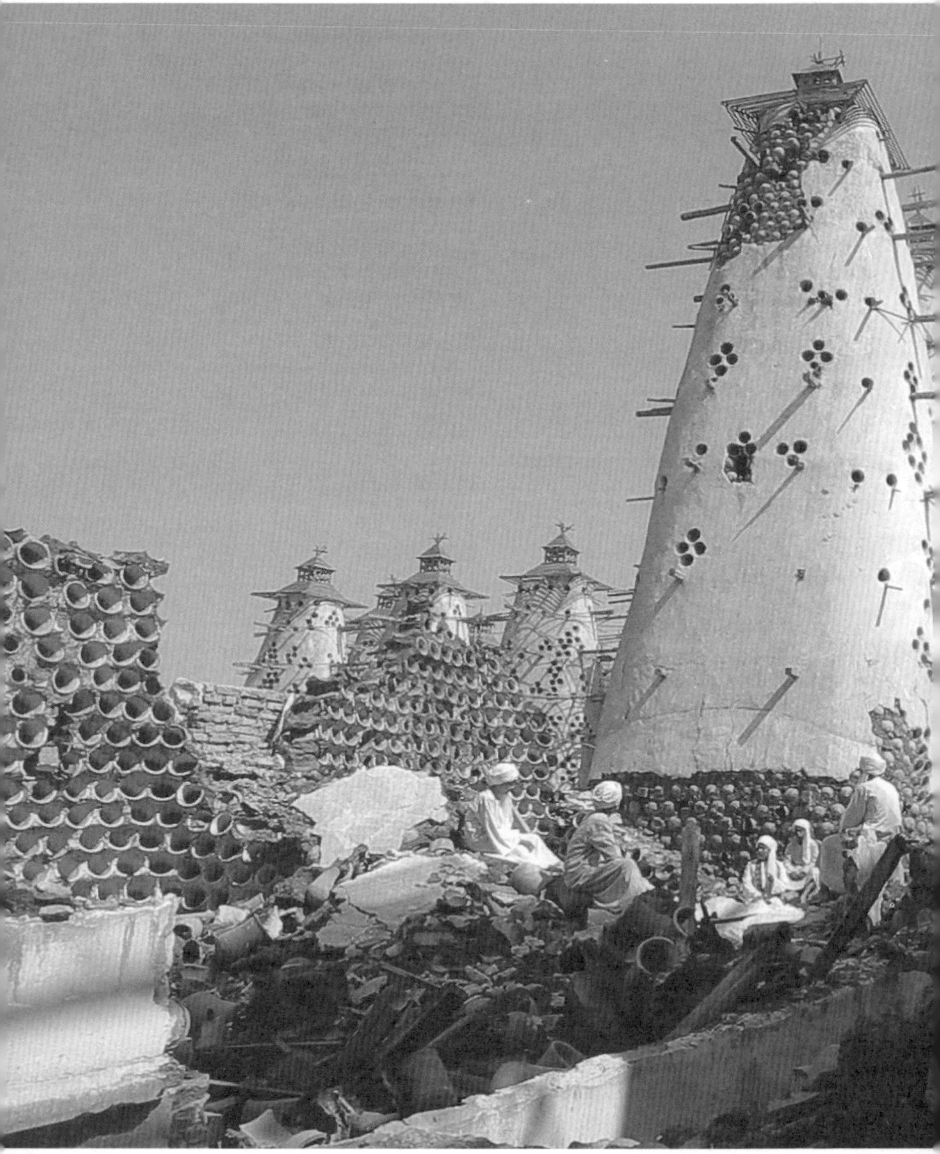